Experiencing
the
Holy Spirit

Other Books by Larry Keefauver

Hugs for Grandparents

Lord, I Wish My Family Would Get Saved

Lord, I Wish My Husband Would Pray with Me

Lord, I Wish My Teenager Would Talk with Me

When God Doesn't Heal Now

Experiencing the Holy Spirit

TRANSFORMED BY HIS PRESENCE

LARRY KEEFAUVER

Publishers Since 1798

THOMAS NELSON PUBLISHERS®
Nashville

To the precious Holy Spirit,

my ever-present Friend

Published in Nashville, Tennessee, by Thomas Nelson, Inc.

Unless otherwise noted, Scripture quotations are from the *Holy Bible,* New Living Translation, copyright © 1996. Used by permission of Tyndale House Publishers, Inc., Wheaton, Illinois 60189. All rights reserved.

Scripture quotations noted NIV are from the HOLY BIBLE: NEW INTERNATIONAL VERSION®. Copyright © 1973, 1978, 1984 by International Bible Society. Used by permission of Zondervan Publishing House. All rights reserved.

Scripture quotations noted KJV are from the KING JAMES VERSION.

Scripture quotations noted NKJV are from THE NEW KING JAMES VERSION. Copyright © 1979, 1980, 1982, Thomas Nelson, Inc., Publishers.

ISBN 0-7852-6976-2

Printed in the United States of America.
1 2 3 4 5 6 — 05 04 03 02 01 00

Contents

Acknowledgments

My deepest gratitude and love for my wife, Judi, who encouraged and persevered through this project.

My heartfelt thanks to the kind and supporting folks at Thomas Nelson, including Rolf, Mike, and Brian.

How grateful I am for all the input and experiences that gave the background to this book from the outreach teams at The Gathering Place Worship Center and Pastor Sam Hinn.

Finally, my thanks for all the prayers and support of the YMCS partners.

Introduction: A Real Person

Growing up, I found it all so confusing! If God is one, then what is the Son's relationship to Him? If the Son now sits on the right hand of God making intercession for us, then how does Jesus live in my heart at the same time? And who in heaven's name is the Holy Ghost (in those days, I heard "Holy Ghost" more than "Holy Spirit")?

As a child, I thought of the Holy Ghost like Casper the friendly ghost. Always there, always helping out, but the Holy Ghost was still apart from me—an apparition without personality or uniqueness. I thought the Spirit was an *it*. How wrong I was!

For years as a pastor, I spoke of the Holy Spirit only at weddings, baptisms, funerals, and the obligatory sermon on pentecost. But as the years passed and the Word continued to dwell richly in me, the distance between us lessened. In fact, He had always been there fulfilling my Savior's promise: "I am with you always, even to the end of the age" (Matt. 28:20). Abiding presence—that became a reality to me, not just a theological abstract. Indwelling Spirit—He became a Friend, Counselor, Comforter, and Teacher even as Jesus had promised He would. The Holy Spirit—*He, not it*—has become my constant companion.

Experiencing the Holy Spirit: Transformed by His Presence—that's what this workbook is about. Our journey together will not be a reproduction of my journey. Your only true guide to the Spirit is God's Word. Yes, I will share with you experiences that I and countless others have had with Him. But you cannot clone another's experience. Your walk in the Spirit will be birthed by Him through His Word.

Jesus gave you the Holy Spirit, so what have you done with Him? Ignore Him and you sentence yourself to a Christian walk filled with striving, doing, trying, and becoming frustrated. Experience the Holy Spirit, and discover for yourself a Christian walk filled with intimacy, prayer, change, growth, power, and trust. In your own strength, you cannot walk the Christian walk. But by the Spirit, you will have the closeness with God to be and do all that He desires of you.

Are you ready? Are you hungry? Are you thirsty? Are you tired of trying to be good and ready to be God's? Are you longing to know Him intimately? Because you are a believer, God's Spirit dwells within you. He's closer than your breath. Breathe on your hand. You cannot see your breath, but it's real and it reveals that life is in you. God has breathed His breath on you. The breath of God is the Holy Spirit. You are alive spiritually. This journey of experiencing the Holy Spirit will free you to allow His breath to fill you, empower you, anoint you, flow in you, speak to you, burn in you, and enliven you in every aspect of your Christian walk.

In this study, you will uncover from the Scripture inspired by the Holy Spirit (2 Tim. 3:16) these key truths:

- The Holy Spirit is always at work within you and in other believers.

- The Holy Spirit pursues an intimate relationship with you, making you holy—body, soul, and spirit.

- The Holy Spirit invites you continually to mature as the new creation you are in Christ Jesus.

- The Holy Spirit always convicts you of sin, comforts you in every circumstance, and communicates the truth of God's Word to you.

- You must receive the gift of the Holy Spirit and seek His gifts to minister through you to others.

- You are bearing the fruit of the Holy Spirit so that the person of Christ might live in and through you as you die to self.

- The Holy Spirit empowers you to witness to Jesus, serve Him and His church, and minister His grace and truth to both the saved and the lost.

As you study *Experiencing the Holy Spirit,* each activity you do will be marked with this symbol: . After completing the exercise, return to reading the content of the lesson. These exercises are designed to help you:

- Explore the Word

- Examine yourself

- Experience the Holy Spirit

Do each exercise for yourself. If you are using this workbook in a small group or class, you will want to share as a group from these exercises. (More detailed instructions for small group leaders are found in the Appendix, "Pointers for Leaders." Follow the pointers found there for effective and meaningful sharing in a small group.)

I recommend that you use the New Living Translation as you study because it is the translation used primarily in this workbook. Furthermore, if you want to focus particularly on the Holy Spirit, you might want to use The Holy Spirit Encounter Bible (Creation House). For further biblical study after completing this workbook, I recommend The Spirit-Filled Study Bible (Thomas Nelson).

Part 1

Meet the Holy Spirit

Week 1

THE BREATH AND WIND OF GOD

I grew up in Ft. Lauderdale, Florida. From my earliest memories, my family spent many wonderful, sunny, lazy days at the beach or around a swimming pool. Before a child started kindergarten, there were swimming lessons. A child had to learn to swim in order to live in south Florida. Occasionally the news would report a child drowning in a pool or in the ocean. Not learning how to swim could be fatal!

The Red Cross taught lifesaving courses. Mouth-to-mouth resuscitation was part of the instruction. We learned that for the person who had drowned (and was at death's door) to come back to life, we had to breathe our breath into him. Doing so required closeness, intimacy, and a willingness on the lifesaver's part to give breath.

By His Spirit, God breathed both life and new life into us. He came close and gave us the gift of physical life: "And the LORD God formed a man's body from the dust of the ground and breathed into it the breath of life. And the man became a living person" (Gen. 2:7). The Hebrew word for the Spirit of God is literally His breath (*ruach*). God's creative breath speaking His word brought us into being. God's Spirit created us with purpose and destiny. When we are born again (John 3:1–7), God's Spirit breathes new life into us.

> The prerequisite for *experiencing the Holy Spirit* is trusting Jesus Christ as your Lord and Savior. The Bible teaches us that the gift of the Holy Spirit is given to us when we repent and receive Jesus: "Each of you must turn from your sins and turn to God, and be baptized in the name of Jesus Christ for the forgiveness of your sins. Then you will receive the gift of the Holy Spirit" (Acts 2:38).

If you have not been born again, then read each of the scriptures at the top of the next page, and check them off as you read them.

- [ ] John 3:16: God gave His only Son to die for you and give you eternal life.

- [ ] John 3:1–8: Being born again is being born of water and the Spirit of God into His kingdom.

- [ ] Romans 3:23: Everyone has sinned and is separated from God by sin.

- [ ] Romans 5:6–11: Jesus died for our sins and delivers us from eternal judgment into eternal life.

- [ ] Romans 10:9–10: Confess that Jesus Christ is Lord and believe that God raised Him from the dead and you will be saved.

- [ ] Romans 10:13: Whoever calls upon the name of the Lord will be saved.

- [ ] Acts 2:38: When you are saved, you receive the gift of the Holy Spirit.

If you have not yet been saved and now know and believe the truth about Jesus Christ as your Lord and Savior, I invite you to pray this prayer:

Lord Jesus, I acknowledge that I am a sinner, and I repent of my sins and receive Your forgiveness. I confess that You, Jesus, are the Son of the living God, and I receive You as my personal Lord and Savior. I surrender my life to You. By faith, I trust You and will obey You. Thank You for saving me. I receive by Your grace the gift of the Holy Spirit. Amen.

As a believer, you have received the wonderful gift of the Holy Spirit who now indwells your life and empowers you to live for Christ. Together we will explore how you can experience the Holy Spirit continually as you walk in His Spirit. Get ready for a powerful, wonderful, spiritual journey of experiencing the Holy Spirit!

This Week's Passage to Memorize

For the Spirit of God has made me, and the breath of the Almighty gives me life. (JOB 33:4)

Day 1: CREATED BY GOD'S SPIRIT

INTRODUCTION

God's Spirit has been intimately involved in your life from the creation of humanity to the moment of your conception. Genesis 1:2 reveals that God's Spirit "hovered" over creation. Then God's Spirit created us, and His breath gives us life (Job 33:4). You may feel as if you never knew Him, but He knows your beginning and all your ways. Before you were aware of Him, you experienced the Holy Spirit. By His Spirit, God fashioned you in the womb and gave you life.

Read aloud Psalm 139:1–18 and emphasize each personal pronoun.
What does this psalm reveal about God's Spirit?

Always There, Always Seeking Us Out for a Relationship

The Holy Spirit is always with us. Even when we are unaware of His presence, He is there. Even if we refuse to acknowledge His involvement in our lives, the truth remains: the Spirit of God is always present and ever seeking us out to draw us into a relationship with Him.

You do not have to find the Holy Spirit; He finds you. You do not have to come to Him; He has already come to you. As near as your breath and as close as your most intimate thought, the Holy Spirit is at work around you all of the time. What He is doing will be the subject of our study the rest of this week.

In the Old Testament, the Holy Spirit never permanently indwelt a person. Although He was ever present, He did not indwell people and continually abide in God's people until pentecost in the New Testament (Acts 2).

EXPLORE THE WORD

The Holy Spirit Is at Work All Around Us

I checked into an expensive hotel one evening and noticed that there were ladders, paint-brushes, and wallpapering tools lining the hall to my room. However, no one was around using them. Early the next morning as I left my room for breakfast, the entire hallway had a new look. Fresh paint and paper graced the corridor. None of the tools remained, but the evidence of the work was there, and the smell of fresh paint and wallpaper paste filled the air. All around me, people had been at work, even though I slept right through it.

God's Spirit is continually at work all around you. He constantly changes and shapes the landscape of your life. You may be unaware of His presence, yet you can see evidences of His work in the lives of others and in your relationships with them.

Each of these scriptures records one way that God's Spirit is at work in the world around you. Read the scripture, and then jot down how the Spirit works.

Exodus 31:3: _____

Judges 14:6: _____

1 Samuel 10:6: _____

2 Samuel 23:2: _____

Job 32:8: _____

Isaiah 11:2: _____

Isaiah 59:21: _____

Ezekiel 36:27: _____

Joel 2:28–29: _____

Zechariah 4:6: _____

EXAMINE YOURSELF

How Is the Holy Spirit at Work in Your Life?

Review the ways the Holy Spirit was at work in the scriptures you just read. How is the Holy Spirit at work around you? Even if you do not know Him well, you may have experienced His presence at work in your life. Check some of the ways you may have experienced Him.

How have you experienced the presence of God's Spirit at work all around you?

☐ Having the knowledge that God created all the universe and me

☐ Sensing His presence when reading the Bible

☐ Feeling near to the Spirit in a time of need or crisis

☐ Fellowshipping in His Spirit when I'm with other believers

☐ Being in awe of His Spirit's presence in worship

☐ Hearing the voice of His Spirit in prayer

☐ Having a sudden insight of truth while reading Scripture

☐ Being led by the Spirit's supernatural peace when facing a decision

☐ Other: _____

The Holy Spirit has always been there, but you may not have been aware of or sensitive to His presence. At times when I am very concentrated on my work, my wife can enter my office, but I am unaware that she's standing there. The fact that I don't sense her presence doesn't change the reality that she's right there close to me. The same is true of the Holy Spirit. Just because you haven't been aware of His presence doesn't alter the truth that He's always there.

What keeps you from experiencing His presence? Circle the things that hinder or distract you from experiencing the Holy Spirit's closeness:

• Fear of losing control to the Spirit

• Ignorance about the Spirit

- Distractions in my life

- Lack of experiencing God in my life

- Misunderstanding who the Spirit is

- Lack of hunger or thirst for His presence

- Other: _____

Whatever builds a wall between you and the Spirit can be removed from your life by repenting and giving attention to your relationship with God. God the Father sits on the throne ruling all of creation (Dan. 7:9), and on His right hand is Jesus Christ, who makes continual intercession for us (Eph. 1:20; Heb. 4:14–16; 9; 10). To comfort, counsel, and reveal all truth to us, Jesus has sent us the Holy Spirit (John 14:26; 16:5–15). The very Spirit of God has come alongside us.

If you desire to have a closer relationship with God's Spirit, then repent of whatever hinders your relationship with Him. Pray this prayer of repentance, inserting in the blank what hinders your relationship with the Spirit:

Lord Jesus, I repent of the hindrance of _____
that has been keeping me from drawing close to the Spirit. Forgive me. Holy Spirit, I welcome You into every aspect and moment of my life. Amen.

EXPERIENCE THE HOLY SPIRIT

Are You Ready for a Deeper Walk with God?

For years I went to church and preached evangelistic sermon after evangelistic sermon. To respond to God in those services, a person got saved—a person gets saved only once— or rededicated his life. I wondered with my people, *Is there more to the Christian walk?* Studying the Word of God together, we discovered that God wants us as believers to grow spiritually moment by moment.

Later we will discover that this journey or process of growing spiritually and maturing in Christ is called sanctification. That is, Jesus is making you holy by the Spirit. We will learn more about that in Week 6.

The Holy Spirit is a person (He), not an it. He is the very real presence of God who never leaves or forsakes us (Heb. 13:5–6) and is always with us (Matt. 28:20). How close are you right now in your relationship with God's Spirit?

📖 **Mark an** *X* **on each line to indicate where your relationship is right now with the Holy Spirit.**

Very close	Very distant

Personal	Impersonal

Intimate	Separated

Through the Spirit, Jesus wants to have a close, intimate, personal relationship with you. Is that something you want in your life?

☐ Yes, I want to grow closer to the Lord and have a deeper walk in the Spirit.

☐ No, I do not have a hunger and thirst for a more intimate relationship with the Spirit.

☐ Other: _____

The Holy Spirit continually seeks you out and invites you to spend time with Him in the Word, worship, prayer, and fellowship. As you go through this workbook, you will learn different ways you can fellowship with the Spirit as the Bible promises: "May the grace of our Lord Jesus Christ, the love of God, and the fellowship of the Holy Spirit be with you all" (2 Cor. 13:13). Just as a relationship with a friend grows with continual contact, conversation, and communion, so your relationship with the Holy Spirit will grow and deepen.

📖 **Read aloud the promise of God in Ephesians 1:13–14. Emphasize the word** *you.*

Today's Review

At the end of each day, I will ask you to review and summarize what you have learned and experienced. Your review will become a daily journal of your growing relationship with the Holy Spirit. You may return often to your previous journal days to see how your relationship with the Holy Spirit has grown and how the Holy Spirit has been at work in your life.

My Daily Walk in the Spirit

Review today's study. Ask God to teach you through the Holy Spirit the truths that you learned and to seal them in your heart. Pray for the Spirit to lead and guide you in applying these truths in your daily walk with Him.

What was the most meaningful thing you learned today?

_____

How has your relationship with the Holy Spirit grown today?

_____

What continues to hinder your intimacy with the Holy Spirit?

_____

Describe one way that the Holy Spirit is at work in the world around you.

_____

Write out the passage to memorize for this week. You may use another translation if you prefer. Practice this passage daily.

_____

Write a prayer inviting God's Spirit to communicate with you, fellowship with you, and teach you all that He wants you to know.

_____

Spiritual Truths

- The Spirit of God created me and gave me life.

- When I was born of the Spirit, I was given the guarantee of eternal life in Christ Jesus.

- The person of the Holy Spirit desires continual communion, fellowship, and relationship with me.

Day 2: FILLED BY GOD'S SPIRIT

INTRODUCTION

A sailboat sits listless in the water waiting for wind to fill its sails. It might float aimlessly on the movement of the water, but it cannot really go anywhere without the wind. Now the captain must hoist the sails and be prepared for the wind when it comes. But the boat doesn't make itself go forward. The wind propels it. The sailboat is completely dependent on the wind for movement and power.

Our lives are much like that sailboat. We are powerless to live the Christian life until we are filled by God's Spirit. Filled by the Spirit, we are gifted and inspired to do these things that are required by God. In our own strength, we helplessly try to live for Christ but find ourselves stumbling with every step.

Before the Holy Spirit filled my life, I desperately tried to set and implement goals in my life without success. Like someone making vain New Year's resolutions, I resolved in my own abilities to pray and read the Bible more, only to miss the mark again and again. In frustration, I tried to follow through on obeying Christ and seeking to please Him, only to fail more than I succeeded. As a result, I became more legalistic with myself and others.

Walking in the Spirit is intended to be not a duty but a joy. Fellowshipping with the Holy Spirit is more than having a scheduled appointment once a day during a prayer or devotional time. It's talking with Him all the time about every decision. It's sharing with Him every joy and disappointment. Such fellowship and communion with God's Spirit are impossible without His filling.

EXPLORE THE WORD

Filled to Serve God

Imagine being commissioned to help build the tabernacle. What an awesome and challenging responsibility that would be! Such a commission was given to Bezalel, son of Uri, grandson of Hur, from the tribe of Judah. God appointed Bezalel to make many of the beautiful crafted artifacts in the tabernacle. Such a job was impossible without the filling of the Holy Spirit.

Read the following scriptures, and then answer the questions.

Read Exodus 31:1–5. What did the filling of the Holy Spirit empower Bezalel to do?

_____

Read Exodus 35:30–33. After Bezalel was filled with the Spirit, what did Moses report about him to God's people?

_____

Read Ephesians 5:18–20. When you are filled with the Spirit, what are you empowered to do?

_____

Through the filling of God's Spirit, you receive purpose, direction, gifting, and empowerment to live the Christian life. It's important for you to hoist the sails of your life and let the wind of God's Spirit fill you and take you to deeper depths and higher heights in Christ than you have ever known.

EXAMINE YOURSELF

Are You Stagnating?

We walked into our house after being gone for a week, and the odor overwhelmed us. The pungent smell of death permeated everything—carpet, drapes, furniture, and the whole atmosphere in our home. We could barely breathe, and our eyes watered from the toxic fumes that engulfed us.

The smell emanated from our air-conditioning ducts. After a strenuous search, we located the source of the terrible smell. A mouse had somehow found its way into our attic, eaten through an air duct, and died there. I will never forget that smell.

Walking in the Spirit produces a sweet aroma in our Christian lives. The apostle Paul wrote, "But thanks be to God, who made us his captives and leads us along in Christ's triumphal procession. Now wherever we go he uses us to tell others about the Lord and to spread the Good News like a sweet perfume. Our lives are a fragrance presented by Christ to God. But this fragrance is perceived differently by those being saved and by those perishing" (2 Cor. 2:14–15). When we are alive in the Spirit, we smell of God—the aroma of life permeates everything and everyone around us. When we stagnate in our spiritual walk, we begin to smell of death!

You don't have to stagnate in your Christian walk. Stagnation leads to lukewarmness and frustration. A stagnated Christian goes through the motions of worship but is never filled with the joy of worship. A stagnated believer prays repetitious prayers but rarely prays from the depths of his spirit. A stagnated follower of Christ obeys out of duty but seldom surrenders radically and wholeheartedly to the leading of God.

Are the sails of your life filled with God's Spirit? Put an X on the line near the word indicating where you are right now.

Empty	Half Full	Filled to Overflowing

Pungent	Odorless	Sweet

The Holy Spirit fills you with the gifts and abilities to do God's will. Your obedience to God is

Burdensome	Dutiful	Enthusiastic

The Holy Spirit inspires you to study the Word and pray. Your study and prayer life in the Spirit are

Boring	Systematic	Exciting

The Holy Spirit fills you with a hunger and thirst for God. Your worship is

Ritualistic	Regular	Joyful

If you find yourself more on the left of center of the continuums instead of toward the right—filled with the Spirit—then invite the Holy Spirit to fill your life to overflowing so that you are moved by the Spirit to live totally surrendered to the Lord in every area of your life—feelings, attitudes, actions, spiritual disciplines, thoughts, and motives.

Write a prayer asking the Holy Spirit to fill those areas of your life that are stagnant, empty, and listless.

_____

_____

_____

Experience the Holy Spirit

Are You Ready to Be Filled by God's Spirit?

Filling requires preparation and willingness. The Holy Spirit never imposes Himself upon you like a puppeteer controlling a puppet. He works with, in, and through you but never without your permission. Throughout the New Testament, we read the reports of what happened when the Holy Spirit filled those early believers. What the Spirit did through them, He will do now through you as long as you are ready and willing.

F. B. Meyer wrote, "The perpetual filling of the Holy Spirit is only possible to those who obey Him, and who obey Him in all things."

Years ago I heard the story of a teacher asking the people in a Bible class if they were willing to be used of God—to go wherever God commanded them to go and to do whatever He asked them to do. One student responded, "I'm not willing yet." To which the teacher responded, "Then, sir, are you willing to be made willing?" Are you willing? Or are you willing to be made willing by the Spirit?

Read each scripture on the next page and then describe what happened after the Spirit filled each believer. Then check "Yes, I am willing," and ask the Holy Spirit to fill and use you this way. Or check "Yes, I'm ready to be made willing," or "No, I'm not willing."

Acts 2:4:

☐ Yes, I am willing.

☐ Yes, I'm ready to be made willing.

☐ No, I'm not willing.

Acts 4:31:

☐ Yes, I am willing.

☐ Yes, I'm ready to be made willing.

☐ No, I'm not willing.

Acts 7:55:

☐ Yes, I am willing.

☐ Yes, I'm ready to be made willing.

☐ No, I'm not willing.

Acts 13:52:

☐ Yes, I am willing.

☐ Yes, I'm ready to be made willing.

☐ No, I'm not willing.

My Daily Walk in the Spirit

Review today's study. If you pictured your walk in the Spirit as a boat on the water, how would you see yourself? Check one.

☐   Dead in the water

☐   Sails up but waiting to be filled

☐   Filled and moving ahead

☐   Rapidly going forward in the Spirit to win the race

☐   Other: _____

When you are filled by the Spirit to accomplish something that you in your own strength could never do, how is your relationship with God deepened and strengthened?

_____

Write out this week's passage to memorize, and circle the part most meaningful to you.

_____

Write a prayer asking the Holy Spirit to fill you.

_____

Spiritual Truths

- The Holy Spirit fills me with His power and ability to do God's will.

- The filling of the Spirit gifts me to accomplish things beyond my natural abilities.

- For the Spirit to fill me, I must be willing or willing to be made willing.

Day 3: Empowered by the Spirit

Introduction

Trying is not trusting. Experiencing the Holy Spirit is not about working and exerting effort to please God. In fact, it's impossible to live the Christian life without His power. God's people discovered this truth in the Old Testament. Every time they tried to do what was right "in their own eyes," everything ended up a disaster. Everything!

D. L. Moody addressed this issue: "Some Christians are interested only in working. They seem to think they are losing time if they wait on God for His power, and away they go to work hard without unction . . . A man working without this unction, this anointing, without the Holy Ghost upon him, is losing time after all."

Time and time again after the Israelites had inhabited the promised land, they fell away from God's will and began to worship idols. Then Israel's enemies in the land, especially the Philistines, rose up and oppressed them: "In those days Israel had no king, so the people did whatever seemed right in their own eyes" (Judg. 17:6). Doing what seemed right, but not being led by the Spirit, left Israel oppressed and defeated.

Have you ever been caught in the endless spiritual cycle in your life of trying to do what you think is right only to be attacked, depressed, and defeated? Without the constant empowering of the Holy Spirit, you will never live a steadfast, victorious Christian life. You and I can't do it by ourselves. We need God's empowerment through His Spirit.

Explore the Word

What Are You Trying to Accomplish in Your Own Strength?

As a pastor, I often tried to minister in my own strength. At times, ministry went great, and I felt wonderful. At other times, attendance was down, the offering was low, or someone in the church complained or even hurt another person. I felt discouraged and set my sights on trying harder to be an effective minister.

Then I tried to be the best husband and father possible. Again, I achieved great successes and bell-ringing defeats. On the spiritual discipline front, for weeks I had joyous quiet times with God, and then for weeks I was completely off course and unresponsive to God. Have you ever been there? Is walking your spiritual walk like being on a roller coaster? It will always be up and down when you try instead of trust, when you do your best to live the Christian life without the Spirit's power.

Read Zechariah 4:6. Rewrite or paraphrase the verse in your own words.

_____

Complete these sentences:

I find myself trying to live the Christian life in my own strength when I

_____

I experience ups and downs in my spiritual walk because I

_____

In the Old Testament, God raised up judges for the people of Israel. God empowered those judges to lead His people out of bondage and back into freedom.

Read the book of Judges about these mighty leaders empowered by the Holy Spirit, and then jot down what God's Spirit empowered them to do.

Othniel (Judg. 3): _____

Gideon (Judg. 6): _____

Jephthah (Judg. 11): _____

Samson (Judg. 13–15):_____

God's Spirit wants to empower you today to do all that God purposes in your life. Read Acts 1:1–8. Write down what these verses say to you about what the Holy Spirit empowers you to do.

_____

_____

EXAMINE YOURSELF

What's Damming Up the Spirit's Power in Your Life?

Where's the power in your life? Empowered by the Spirit, the judges provided leadership to a wayward nation. Where is the Holy Spirit empowering your life? In what areas of your life do you still try to exercise control?

Repentance and confession precede empowerment. Only when we acknowledge our weakness, sin, and failings can we receive the power of the Holy Spirit to change and strengthen our lives. Read 2 Corinthians 12:9–10.

Repent to God. The greatest dam holding back the river of the Spirit's power in my life is

_____

Confess to God. I confess that my weakness is

_____

I believed my preaching to be strong, but when I recognized just how poor my preaching was without the Holy Spirit, my weak preaching became the tool for the Spirit to use to witness and to disciple. In your own strength, whatever you accomplish is lacking compared to what He can do through you.

EXPERIENCE THE HOLY SPIRIT

Where Are You Being Empowered by the Holy Spirit?

We read earlier in this study that the reason the Spirit pours out His power on us is to make us bold witnesses and disciples for the gospel. When the lost who know your weaknesses see you live the Christian life in spite of those failings, the power of the gospel to change, transform, deliver, heal, and overcome becomes evident to them. It's called *power evangelism.* The power of the Spirit is demonstrated in you, attracting the lost to Jesus.

The Spirit's power may also work through you in supernatural ways. In the early disciples and followers of Jesus, the Spirit's power was demonstrated in miracles, signs, wonders, salvations, spiritual gifts, boldness, and mighty, supernatural works.

Complete these sentences:

One way I am experiencing the Spirit's power is

_____

I need to experience the Spirit's power in

_____

MY DAILY WALK IN THE SPIRIT

As you review today's study, surrender your strength to the Spirit's power. Pray this prayer:

Almighty God, You are strong, and I am weak. Spirit of God, You are my Helper, for I am helpless. I can do all things through Christ who strengthens me. Without Your Spirit, I can do nothing. Spirit of God, empower me to be a bold witness. Use me as a vessel of Your wonder-working power in my life. Amen.

List the areas of surrender in your life where the Spirit's power is free to flow.

_____

List the areas of trying in your life that need to be transformed by the Spirit into trusting.

_____

Describe where the dams must break within you to allow the river of the Spirit's power to flow out of you.

_____

SPIRITUAL TRUTHS

- The Holy Spirit empowers me to do mighty things beyond my own abilities.

- Repentance and confession demolish the dams within me that hold back the rivers of the Spirit's power.

- The Holy Spirit empowers me to be a bold witness of the gospel and to be a vessel of His signs, wonders, miracles, and mighty works.

Day 4: Prophesied by the Spirit

Introduction

God's word (the Hebrew *davar*) is both what He says and what He does. Everything God says, He does. And all that He does is His word to us. When the Spirit of God came upon a prophet in the Old Testament, that prophet (*nabi*) became a mouthpiece of God's word to His people. At times, the prophets foretold what God would do, but usually they forth-told God's words of warning, judgment, exhortation, and edification.

The Holy Spirit inspired the prophets to speak God's word to others. People prophesy by the Spirit today as well. They proclaim and preach God's word—boldly forthtelling what God is saying to our day and generation. At times, a prophet may foretell what God will do if we obey His word or fail to obey His word.

Almost a decade ago, I was struggling with some of the unorthodox decisions of my denomination. In a dramatic way, the Holy Spirit spoke into my life as I raked leaves in our backyard on a Thanksgiving Day. The Holy Spirit prophetically spoke into my life to leave where I was and to follow His leading into a new direction for me and for my family.

I had been in my denomination since birth. I had never known another type of church or style of worship. I had become comfortable or stagnant in my spiritual walk. The Spirit began to speak prophetically into my life through the lives of a men's Bible study group. The Holy Spirit confirmed the direction of my life through His word, His voice, and through speaking to me through the lives of other believers.

EXPLORE THE WORD

How Did the Spirit Speak?

The prophets spoke God's word throughout history by the inspiration of the Holy Spirit. Peter wrote, "It was the Holy Spirit who moved the prophets to speak from God" (2 Peter 1:21). God reveals Himself to us in many ways. Through dreams, visions, circumstances, creation, people, and the Scripture, God's Spirit speaks to us.

Check the ways you have heard the Spirit's voice:

☐ God's Word   ☐ Dreams and visions

☐ Still, small voice in me   ☐ Circumstances

☐ Creation   ☐ Other: _____

The Holy Spirit spoke through the Old Testament prophets to reveal God to us.

Read each of the passages, and summarize how God's Spirit spoke.

1 Samuel 10:6–10: _____

1 Samuel 19:23: _____

1 Chronicles 12:18: _____

2 Chronicles 24:20: _____

Ezekiel 2:2; 11:5: _____

Micah 3:8: _____

Zechariah 7:12: _____

God's Spirit still speaks prophetically to us today.

📖 Read 1 Corinthians 14, and list all the ways the Holy Spirit speaks today in the church.

_____

_____

God promised through the Old Testament prophet Joel that He would pour out His Spirit on all flesh so that they might prophesy. At pentecost that prophecy was fulfilled.

📖 Read Joel 2:28 and Acts 1:1–8. Summarize how the Holy Spirit will be poured out in the last days.

_____

_____

EXAMINE YOURSELF

What Has the Spirit Spoken to You?

Hearing the voice of God's Spirit requires that every other voice within us be silenced. In 1 Kings, we read that God's voice is gentle and quiet: "After the earthquake there was a fire, but the LORD was not in the fire. And after the fire there was the sound of a gentle whisper. When Elijah heard it, he wrapped his face in his cloak and went out and stood at the entrance of the cave. And a voice said, 'What are you doing here, Elijah?'" (1 Kings 19:12–13).

Hearing the Spirit's voice speak prophetically to us and through us requires the disciplines of both obedience and silence. We must silence every other voice within and around us that vies for our attention. God's Spirit refuses to compete with any other voice or distraction in our lives. He demands our full attention. Does He have yours? What voices keep you from hearing the Spirit's voice?

Check all the voices that need to be silenced within you so that you might hear the Spirit speak to you as He spoke to prophets of old or to the early church believers:

- [ ] Worldly voices
- [ ] The voices of others who are doubters and skeptics
- [ ] My voice
- [ ] Satan's voice
- [ ] Other: _____

Are you willing to silence all other voices including your own so that you might hear the Spirit speak prophetically into your life?

EXPERIENCE THE HOLY SPIRIT

Will You Be Still and Know Him?

If you are to know God's Spirit, you must wait and listen for Him. Does your daily schedule permit you to spend time in the presence of the Holy Spirit?

Read Psalms 37:7 and 46:10.

Consider your daily schedule. When do you have time to be still and silent? When will you listen to the Holy Spirit speak into your life prophetically—foretelling and forthtelling God's word?

Experiencing the Holy Spirit requires abandonment of worldly concerns and detachment from every distraction. Get alone with the Spirit. Immerse yourself in God's Word. Pray intently and intensely. Listen. Wait to hear His voice.

My Daily Walk in the Spirit

Begin your review of today's study by saying aloud this week's memory passage, and then sitting in silence for at least fifteen minutes. Set aside every thought but the thought of Christ and His love for you. Listen quietly for the voice of His Spirit.

The Holy Spirit has prophetically spoken to me, saying:

_____

In the future, the time I will spend daily listening to His Spirit will be

_____

What distracts me most from hearing the Spirit's voice is

_____

Write down a verse from today's study that you will memorize and hide in your heart.

_____

Write a prayer thanking God for all the ways the Spirit has spoken to you in the past.

_____

Spiritual Truths

- God's Spirit speaks to me.

- When the Holy Spirit speaks, I must silence all other voices in order to hear His.

- To listen to His voice, I must be still in His presence.

Day 5: Anointed by the Spirit

Introduction

In Scripture, one of the symbols of the Holy Spirit is oil. When oil is rubbed into or poured on, the Bible calls this action "to anoint." And prophetically the Old Testament prophecies foretell of an Anointed One (in the Hebrew, *Messiah*) who will come and save God's people.

📖 **Read Isaiah 61:1–3.**

The Holy Spirit anointed people for ministry in the Old Testament. Furthermore, the Holy Spirit anointed Jesus, in particular, to be the Anointed One, who would deliver us from sin and death. When Jesus began His earthly ministry, He announced that He is the Messiah (Anointed One) by reading Isaiah 61 in the synagogue at Nazareth (Luke 4). The Greek word for "Anointed One" is *Christ* (*Christos*). Jesus is the Anointed One, the Christ, who pours out on us the oil of the Holy Spirit so that we become Christians—little anointed ones.

Explore the Word

Who Is Anointed with the Spirit?

In the Old Testament, special people were anointed with oil to symbolize their office and to symbolize the Spirit's presence in their lives. Prophets, kings, and priests were anointed. Jesus fulfilled all these offices in Himself as the King, Priest, and Prophet of our lives. Jesus pours out the anointing of the Spirit upon us so that as believers, we might be a royal priesthood and a holy nation (1 Peter 2:9).

📖 **Read each of the following passages, and write down how it describes the anointing of the Holy Spirit.**

Exodus 30:31–33:_____

Exodus 29:4–7; Numbers 3:3:_____

1 Samuel 16:13:_____

Numbers 11:25:_____

The potential exists in your Christian life for the anointing of the Holy Spirit to make you a king, priest, and prophet in the kingdom of God. Are you ready?

EXAMINE YOURSELF

Are You Anointed?

The anointing of the Holy Spirit is the oil of His presence poured out in your life by Christ. The Spirit's anointing transforms you into His image so that your life will mirror the life of Jesus.

📖 **Read 2 Corinthians 3:18.** Rewrite it in your own words, and describe how God's Spirit is working in your life to transform you from glory to glory.

_____

The writers of the Old Testament expectantly awaited the coming of the Messiah, the Anointed One. As we will explore next week, Jesus lived out what an anointed life looks like. He was the Word made flesh (John 1). As a human being, Jesus the Anointed One gave us the example of what an anointed life says, does, thinks, feels, and lives abundantly. His life's purpose was summarized by the anointing of the Spirit described in Isaiah 11:2 and 61:1–3.

📖 **Complete the checklist of anointing at the top of the next page.** Here is a list of some of the qualities of anointing that were on the Messiah's life and that also mark the life of anyone following Jesus the Christ and being transformed by the Spirit. Check off the qualities of anointing that you have experienced in your life.

- [ ] Wisdom
- [ ] Understanding
- [ ] Counsel
- [ ] Might
- [ ] Knowledge

- [ ] Fear of the Lord
- [ ] Taking good news to the poor
- [ ] Comforting the brokenhearted
- [ ] Announcing release to the captives
- [ ] Setting the prisoners free

EXPERIENCE THE HOLY SPIRIT

Will You Pray for the Anointing of the Holy Spirit?

The Holy Spirit desires to anoint you for ministry and service. You can live the Christlike, Spirit-filled life, which is anointed for His glory. Jesus promised,

> I tell you, keep on asking, and you will be given what you ask for. Keep on looking, and you will find. Keep on knocking, and the door will be opened. For everyone who asks, receives. Everyone who seeks, finds. And the door is opened to everyone who knocks. You fathers—if your children ask for a fish, do you give them a snake instead? Or if they ask for an egg, do you give them a scorpion? Of course not! If you sinful people know how to give good gifts to your children, how much more will your heavenly Father give the Holy Spirit to those who ask him. (LUKE 11:9–13)

Are you willing to ask for the Holy Spirit? You will not experience Him unless you ask for His anointing in your life. Jesus promised that if you ask, you will receive.

Not receiving the Holy Spirit in your life is like having a special and important guest staying in your home but never inviting him out of the guest room. Yes, he is living in your house, but you never invite him to talk with you, dine with you, or share with you in the other rooms of your home. You may have been a Christian for years but never invited the Holy Spirit to enter all the rooms of your heart. Yes, He lives within the secret place, the Holy of Holies, within your life, but the rest of your life remains shut up to His anointing.

You can ask the Holy Spirit to pour out Himself into every area of your life. Will you pray for His anointing?

📖 **Write a brief prayer asking for the Holy Spirit to enter into and anoint these areas of your life.**

Family:

_____

Work:

_____

Study:

_____

Relationships:

_____

Feelings:

_____

Thoughts:

_____

Actions:

_____

Know that the Holy Spirit will enter in, transform, and make holy every area of your life. And He will continue to convict you about sin in the areas you don't invite Him into, and He will expose these areas to His light.

The Holy Spirit stands knocking at every locked door in your life. What is hidden, He brings to light. What is sin, He brings to repentance. What is lost, He finds. What is unknown, He teaches. Ask for His anointing to pour out and be rubbed into all of your life.

My Daily Walk in the Spirit

Review what you have learned about and experienced in the Holy Spirit today. Complete these sentences:

The area of my life most anointed by the Spirit is

_____

The area of my life that has been closed off to the Spirit is

_____

What I am asking of the Spirit is

_____

Write a brief diary of how the Holy Spirit has been at work *in* your life this week.

_____

Write a prayer thanking God for all the ways you are experiencing the Holy Spirit.

_____

Write down the passage to memorize for this week.

_____

Spiritual Truths

- The Holy Spirit anointed Jesus as the Anointed One—King, Priest, and Prophet.

- The Holy Spirit is transforming me into the likeness of Jesus Christ.

- I can experience the anointing of the Holy Spirit in my life by asking the Spirit into every area of my life and relationships.

Week 2

THE SPIRIT-LED JESUS

Growing up in the church, I continually had questions about how I could live the Christian life. It seemed so hard to be good, spiritual, holy, and loving all the time. In fact, the more I read the Bible and went to Sunday school, the more frustrated I became because I knew I couldn't do all that Jesus wanted me to do. Reading the Sermon on the Mount convinced me it was impossible to do all that Jesus commanded.

So I asked lots of questions. One of the real puzzles that perplexed me was how Jesus could "live in my heart." Obviously Jesus walked the earth as a man and died on the cross. Then God raised Jesus from the dead, and He ascended into heaven where He sits on the right hand of God. How does Jesus also then live in my heart? I had images as a child of this full-grown man trying to squeeze into my child's small heart. Teachers told me just to accept it by faith. Then a teacher tried to explain the Trinity, and my faith was stretched again with difficult concepts to understand.

Finally someone explained to me how the Son sent the Holy Spirit to baptize, immerse, fill, indwell, and anoint us so that we could live the Christian life. It was easier to understand a Spirit indwelling me, but I was far from out of the woods in understanding the Spirit-led life. I confess that even though I have had years of theological training and read hundreds of books on the Trinity and the Holy Spirit, not all my questions are answered. There are still many mysteries about the Holy Spirit. But I know this: without Him, it's impossible to be like Jesus. Without the indwelling and abiding Holy Spirit, it's impossible to understand and apply God's Word, much less obey His commands.

This week, we will explore together how Jesus, the Anointed One, who was conceived by and filled with the Spirit, lived a Spirit-led example. His life demonstrates two things for us:

1. It's possible to follow, obey, love, and be like Jesus through the Spirit.

2. The Holy Spirit is making us more and more like Jesus every day.

From the moment of His conception, Jesus was anointed by the Holy Spirit. Jesus was always intimate with the Holy Spirit because His very nature was both divine and human. As the Anointed One (Christ or Messiah), Jesus was led, empowered, and continually filled with the Holy Spirit. Let me share with you something very exciting. The moment you are born again, the nature of Jesus Christ is birthed in you. You become a new creation in Christ—the Anointed One. Paul wrote, "Therefore, if anyone is in Christ, he is a new creation; the old has gone, the new has come!" (2 Cor. 5:17 NIV).

The Holy Spirit has birthed in you a new nature. Christ's Spirit lives in you and empowers you to live the Christian life. Paul declared, "I myself no longer live, but Christ lives in me. So I live my life in this earthly body by trusting in the Son of God, who loved me and gave himself for me" (Gal. 2:20).

What does a Christian life look like? It mirrors the life of Jesus. His character, nature, and ministry have been birthed in you, and you will live forever. Nicodemus asked Jesus, "How can an old man go back into his mother's womb and be born again?" Jesus replied, "The truth is, no one can enter the Kingdom of God without being born of water and the Spirit. Humans can reproduce only human life, but the Holy Spirit gives new life from heaven. So don't be surprised at my statement that you must be born again. Just as you can hear the wind but can't tell where it comes from or where it is going, so you can't explain how people are born of the Spirit" (John 3:4–8).

Good news. Like Jesus, you can live the Spirit-led life because as a believer, you are born of the Spirit. I've heard some Christians say, "You can never be like Jesus." But Jesus says, "Follow Me." He has given us the power to follow Him and live like Him through the Holy Spirit. Let's discover how.

This Week's Passage to Memorize

He is the Holy Spirit, who leads into all truth. The world at large cannot receive him, because it isn't looking for him and doesn't recognize him. But you do, because he lives with you now and later will be in you. (JOHN 14:17)

Day 1: THE SPIRIT'S LEADING

INTRODUCTION

Have you ever been directed someplace you didn't want to go? I was directed to a gym to get in shape and lose weight. I was directed to a surgeon when my family doctor determined that my appendix needed to be removed. I was directed to a dental surgeon when my wisdom teeth needed to come out. All of that direction led to short-term pain for a long-term gain. Needless to say, I wasn't excited about going in any of those directions, but I knew that each leading was in my best interests.

The Holy Spirit leads us where God wants us to go for our eternal benefit. At times, the immediate impact on us may be trying, testing, difficult, or even painful.

> 📖 **Read Romans 5:3–5.**

The Holy Spirit led Jesus into a time of trial and testing called the wilderness. There Christ was strengthened as the Holy Spirit filled Him with the Father's love and power to resist Satan.

EXPLORE THE WORD

Has the Spirit Ever Led You into the Wilderness?

If you are to experience the Holy Spirit, you must go where He leads you. You will never desperately thirst for the living water of the Spirit (John 7:39) until you follow Him into the desert of spiritual dryness. At times the Spirit leads you through a wilderness so that you might learn to depend solely on Him. Many have not experienced the Holy Spirit simply because they refuse to admit their spiritual desperation and poverty.

How desperate are you for the Spirit? How hungry are you for His will? The Spirit led Jesus into the wilderness. Matthew wrote, "Then Jesus was led out into the wilderness by the Holy Spirit to be tempted there by the Devil" (Matt. 4:1). However, Mark described the situation this way: "Immediately the Holy Spirit compelled Jesus to go into the wilderness" (Mark 1:12).

Read Matthew 4:1–11; Mark 1:12–13; and Luke 4:1–13. Answer the following questions:

What important spiritual tests and revelations did Jesus encounter in the wilderness?

_____

_____

How was Jesus strengthened in being led by the Spirit into the wilderness?

_____

_____

Read the following verses and describe how Jesus was led by the Spirit.

Luke 4:14–44: Led by the Spirit, Jesus did the following things (list all that He was led and empowered by the Spirit to do):

_____

_____

_____

EXAMINE YOURSELF

How Do You Respond When the Spirit Leads?

The Holy Spirit led Jesus to sick and hurting people, dying people, angry and demon-possessed people. The Spirit led Jesus to villages and crowded places, lonely and desolate places, and the most painful of places—the wilderness, Gethsemane, and Calvary.

How do you respond? When the Holy Spirit leads you into such places and to such people, what will your response be? (Turn to the next page and check the word or phrase that describes how you usually respond to trials, testings, problems, and difficult situations.)

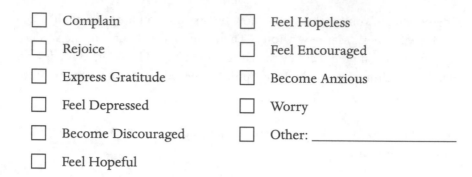

☐ Complain   ☐ Feel Hopeless

☐ Rejoice   ☐ Feel Encouraged

☐ Express Gratitude   ☐ Become Anxious

☐ Feel Depressed   ☐ Worry

☐ Become Discouraged   ☐ Other: _____

☐ Feel Hopeful

Will your usual response be your probable response? If you used to respond negatively to trials but now you don't, how is the Holy Spirit shaping your character and changing you? If you still respond negatively, when will you let the Spirit change you?

 **Check the words that describe where you are right now in your spiritual walk (based on Rom. 5:3–5).**

I am experiencing . . .

☐ Pain and Suffering   ☐ Strength of Character

☐ Trial   ☐ Confident Expectation (Hope)

☐ Endurance   ☐ Heart Filled with Love

EXPERIENCE THE HOLY SPIRIT

Are You Desperate Enough to Ask?

Jesus asked to be baptized. In response to His asking, the Holy Spirit both baptized and descended upon Him. It was a defining moment in Jesus' life. The Spirit defined Him as God's Son and led Him into testing. Through repentance and baptism, you have been defined as a "child of God" (John 1:12–13). Will you be desperate enough for God's leading that you will follow wherever the Spirit leads—even into the wilderness?

Oswald Chambers wrote,

> Ask if you have not received. There is nothing more difficult than asking. We will have yearnings and desires for certain things, and even suffer as a result of their going unfulfilled, but not until we are at the limit of desperation will we *ask*. It is the sense of not being spiritually real that causes us to ask. Have you ever asked out of the depth of your total insufficiency and poverty? . . . The best thing to do, once you are not spiritually real, is to ask God for the Holy Spirit . . . The Holy Spirit is the one who makes everything that Jesus did for you real in your life. (*My Utmost for His Highest* [Nashville, TN: Thomas Nelson Publishers, 1992], June 9)

Describe how desperate you are, how thirsty you are, how hungry you are for the Holy Spirit.

_____

_____

To be led by the Spirit means you must be desperate enough to follow Christ anywhere!

MY DAILY WALK IN THE SPIRIT

 Review what you have learned and experienced in the Spirit. Describe how spiritually real your life is right now.

_____

In the future, how will you respond—by the Spirit's power—to trials and tests, wildernesses and deserts in your life?

_____

How has being led by the Spirit into trials and tests strengthened your character and filled you with hope and the Spirit's love?

_____

Write a prayer committing to God that you will go wherever the Spirit leads.

_____

Write down the passage to memorize for this week.

_____

SPIRITUAL TRUTHS

- The Holy Spirit led Jesus and will lead me into trials and tests in the wilderness.

- When I become dry and thirsty enough to ask for Him, Jesus will fill me with the Spirit.

- I can be led by the Spirit, just as Jesus was, to do mighty things for God's glory.

Day 2: THE SPIRIT FILLS WITH POWER AND JOY

INTRODUCTION

When I couldn't do all that I knew God required of me, I felt burdened and overwhelmed in my spiritual walk. Have you ever been there? I had Christian responsibilities to fulfill as a husband, father, worker, and Christian leader. Too much to do and not enough time was my life's melody played out on the minor chords of a troubled spirit. Powerless Christian living leads a sour, doleful existence. Are you bubbling over with joy or just a pain to be around?

What was the source of Jesus' power? Where did He get the power to do all of His mighty miracles, healings, and deliverances? Luke explained, "Then Jesus returned to Galilee, filled with the Holy Spirit's power" (Luke 4:14). Jesus was empowered by the Holy Spirit to do all that He did.

Where do you get your power and strength? Is your Christian life Spirit led or burden filled? Despite all the suffering Jesus saw and the persecution He faced, Jesus was "filled with the joy of the Holy Spirit" (Luke 10:21). Is your life filled with joy or the drudgery of duty and obligation?

EXPLORE THE WORD

Are You Joyfully Walking in the Spirit's Power?

Your spiritual walk can be one of power and joy! Empowered by the Spirit, you can do and say things that are supernatural. Jesus promised, "The truth is, anyone who believes in me will do the same works I have done, and even greater works, because I am going to be with the Father. You can ask for anything in my name, and I will do it, because the work of the Son brings glory to the Father" (John 14:12–13).

Let's explore Jesus' ministry and see how the Spirit empowered Him to do God's will.

Everything He did and said came from the Father. Jesus said, "Don't you believe that I am in the Father and the Father is in me? The words I say are not my own, but my Father who lives in me does his work through me" (John 14:10).

> **Read these scriptures, and describe what Jesus did and promised to us through the power and joy of the Spirit.**

Matthew 10:20; Mark 13:11: _____

Matthew 2:18:_____

Matthew 12:28:_____

Mark 1:8:_____

Luke 4:18: _____

Luke 10:21: _____

Luke 24:49: _____

John 6:63: _____

John 7:39: _____

John 14:17: _____

John 16:15: _____

The Holy Spirit filled Jesus with power and joy to do the will of His Father. The Holy Spirit also fills you with the same power and joy to do God's will.

EXAMINE YOURSELF

Are You Living in the Spirit's Power?

You have just read Jesus' promise that out of the Spirit living within us would flow fountains of living water (John 7:39). So are the joy and power of His Spirit bubbling like a fountain out of you? Or do you feel burdened, helpless, and oppressed in your spiritual walk?

A woman shared with me her struggles. She felt like a failure as a wife and mom. Actually she was a loving wife and mother who was very conscientious in all her responsibilities. But whenever she fell short of her or her family's expectations, she put herself under heavy condemnation. As a result, she didn't walk in power and joy. She wasn't seeing the fruit of the

Holy Spirit in her life; rather, she saw only her shortcomings. She was not experiencing the Holy Spirit's power to live for Christ.

📖 **Read aloud Romans 8:1–2, inserting your name in verse 2.**

The greatest destroyer of power and joy in your spiritual walk is condemnation. Condemnation comes from the accuser—Satan (Rev. 12:10–12). The Spirit will convict you of sin and lead you to repentance, but He will never condemn you.

EXPERIENCE THE HOLY SPIRIT

Will You Walk in the Power, Joy, and Liberty of the Holy Spirit?

Walking in the power of the Spirit means that the power of sin is broken in your life. Condemnation has no place in your thoughts. Like Jesus, you can say and do what the Father tells you to say and do.

📖 **Describe what the Father is telling you to say and do now in your life.**

_____

_____

When you feel powerless due to condemnation in your life, take these steps in the Spirit:

- Examine your heart, confessing any sinful habit, attitude, thought, or action in your life.

- Spend time in God's Word, especially reading Psalms 51 and 103.

- Fellowship with Christians who build you up and don't tear you down (Ps. 1).

- Refuse to believe the lie of the accuser that you are guilty. The truth is that you are forgiven (1 John 1:9).

- Ask God to fill you with the power and joy of the Holy Spirit.

MY DAILY WALK IN THE SPIRIT

Review what you have learned and experienced in the Spirit today.

Describe how you are walking in the power of the Spirit.

_____

In what will you rejoice today?

_____

What steps do you need to take to rebuke condemnation and walk in the life-giving power of the Holy Spirit?

_____

Write a prayer confessing any sin that hinders you and thanking God for forgiving you and freeing you from condemnation.

_____

Write this week's passage to memorize.

_____

SPIRITUAL TRUTHS

- I can walk in the power and joy of the Holy Spirit, just as Jesus did.

- I can do what my Father asks me to do in the Spirit's power.

- I am free from condemnation and free to experience the life-giving power of the Holy Spirit.

Day 3: DON'T REJECT THE HOLY SPIRIT

INTRODUCTION

All of my life I have heard that the one unforgivable sin is to blaspheme the Holy Spirit. Of course, in a sense the second unforgivable sin is to be unforgiving (Matt. 6:15). Jesus warned, "I assure you of this: If anyone acknowledges me publicly here on earth, I, the Son of Man, will openly acknowledge that person in the presence of God's angels. But if anyone denies me here on earth, I will deny that person before God's angels. Yet those who speak against the Son of Man may be forgiven, but anyone who speaks blasphemies against the Holy Spirit will never be forgiven" (Luke 12:8–10).

To blaspheme the Holy Spirit is to reject Jesus Himself. Everything the Spirit says and does points to Jesus (John 15:26). To blaspheme the Spirit is to reject His presence in your life. And Jesus sent Him to give us new birth. Unless we are born again, we cannot receive the gift of eternal life and be with Jesus forever.

EXPLORE THE WORD

How Precious Is the Spirit?

Jesus places ultimate importance on the presence of the Holy Spirit in our lives. Without the Spirit, we cannot know Jesus. He reveals Jesus to us and teaches us all about Him. The Spirit is so precious to Jesus that some of the strongest warnings in the Bible pertain to rejecting the Holy Spirit.

> **Read Matthew 12:22–32 and Luke 12:8–10.** Answer the questions at the top of the next page.

By what power does Jesus cast out demons?

_____

What sin cannot be forgiven?

_____

How should we regard the Holy Spirit in our lives?

_____

EXAMINE YOURSELF

How Precious Is the Holy Spirit to You?

When do you speak or think about the Holy Spirit? When you do speak about the Holy Spirit, do you give Him the honor and respect that you give the Father and the Son? So dear and precious was the Holy Spirit to Jesus that rejecting Him meant rejecting Jesus.

When you speak about or think about the Holy Spirit, how do you refer to Him?

Check those that apply to you:

☐ I speak lovingly to Him.   ☐ I never talk about Him.

☐ I speak of Him as an _it_.   ☐ I don't know how to refer to Him.

☐ It's hard for me to think about the Holy Spirit as a person.

☐ Other: _____

Think for a moment about marriage. Two people become one in Christ. Is it possible to reject the wife without rejecting the husband? Of course not. Imagine having a dinner party for couples and inviting the husband without inviting the wife. Such an invitation would be very offensive. The same is true with the Holy Spirit. Inviting Jesus to be Lord and Savior of our lives is also inviting the Holy Spirit to indwell us. We cannot have Jesus without the accompanying Holy Spirit.

Write down how you feel about the Holy Spirit.

EXPERIENCE THE HOLY SPIRIT

Will You Tell Him?

You may have told the Father and the Son about your love and devotion. But how often do you speak directly to the Holy Spirit about your love and devotion to Him? He is the person of the Trinity who abides continually with you. Do not ignore Him. Tell Him how you feel.

 Write a prayer expressing your love and devotion to the Holy Spirit. It may be as simple as praying,

Father, I love You. Jesus, I love You. Holy Spirit, I love You.

My Daily Walk in the Spirit

Review today's study. Remember to express your love to the Holy Spirit today.

Describe all the ways in the past that you have spoken about the person of the Holy Spirit.

_____

Write a prayer asking the Holy Spirit to give you the words you need to talk about Him with others.

_____

List all the words that come to your mind to describe the person of the Holy Spirit.

_____

Write down the passage to memorize for this week.

_____

Spiritual Truths

- I can never blaspheme the Spirit by rejecting Him or Jesus.

- I can show my love and devotion to the Holy Spirit just as I do for the Father and the Son.

- Daily the Holy Spirit desires a loving, intimate relationship with me.

Day 4: Meet the Paraclete

Introduction

Jesus named the Holy Spirit the Paraclete—Counselor, Comforter, the One who comes alongside us. In conferences around the country when I share about the Holy Spirit, I often ask a person to stand right beside me and link arms with me. I tell the listeners that the one by my side is the Paraclete.

At first, I walk, talk, and make decisions dragging the Paraclete (the Holy Spirit) around with me. I never notice Him. He is tagging along without any input, say, or counsel. Do you ever treat the Holy Spirit that way? Yes, He's with you, by your side, but you never really notice Him or give Him any attention. You go about living your life, your own way, without any regard for the Holy Spirit.

Of course, my dragging around another person looks humorous to the audience. But there's nothing funny about dragging the Holy Spirit through life as if He's just excess baggage in my life.

Then I ask the person (the Holy Spirit) to take control of me. I promise not to make any decision and not to go in any direction without His leading. Now the person by my side speaks, and I listen. He nudges me in the direction I should go, and I follow His lead. The One beside me truly becomes my Counselor, Guide, and Teacher.

Explore the Word

Are You Listening to the Holy Spirit?

Jesus knew we couldn't live without Him, without His omnipresent Spirit with us to

47

guide and direct us. So He gave us the Holy Spirit. The question confronting you is, Are you listening to the Spirit?

📖 **Read John 14:15–16.** Write down all the revelations Jesus gives about who the Spirit is and what He does in your life.

_____

_____

_____

In Week 7, we will probe deeper into Jesus' teachings about the Holy Spirit. For now, it's important for you to recognize His presence in your life. It's time to build a relationship with Him. He is speaking to you about everything in your life. Are you listening?

Jesus spoke a number of times about how He has given you the Holy Spirit. Just to confirm that the Spirit is with you, read how Jesus has given the Spirit.

📖 **Read each text, and write down how Jesus gave the Holy Spirit to us.**

Matthew 28:19: _____

Mark 13:11; Luke 12:12:_____

Luke 24:49: _____

John 20:22: _____

Acts 1:1–8:_____

EXAMINE YOURSELF

How Do You Respond to the Spirit's Counsel?

Jesus promised, "And I will ask the Father, and he will give you another Counselor, who will never leave you. He is the Holy Spirit, who leads into all truth" (John 14:16–17). When the Holy Spirit begins to lead you into all truth, how do you receive what He says? Jesus further teaches in John 14:17 that the world cannot receive Him or what He says, but how about you?

At times, His counsel will be correction, rebuke, conviction, or admonition. When the Spirit's counsel is correcting, how do you respond? (Circle the response you most commonly have.)

- Anger

- Surprise

- Defensiveness

- Hurt

- Brokenness

- Repentance

- Gratefulness

- Other: _____

At times, the Holy Spirit will encourage and affirm you. But at other times, He may correct and admonish you. The attitude He desires no matter what He counsels is complete surrender and receptiveness to how He is leading. Nothing short of total surrender will meet His will for your response.

EXPERIENCE THE HOLY SPIRIT

Begin Talking to the Spirit

The Holy Spirit is right by your side. Don't delay. Begin talking with Him about everything—your decisions, feelings, goals, frustrations, problems, joys, and more. Don't hold anything back from Him. Remember that you must invite Him to talk to you or lead you. He will not impose Himself on you. When you invite, He comes and leads.

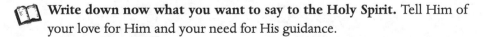 **Write down now what you want to say to the Holy Spirit.** Tell Him of your love for Him and your need for His guidance.

_____

The Holy Spirit will counsel you in everything if you will only listen to Him. Acknowledge His presence, and respond to His voice.

MY DAILY WALK IN THE SPIRIT

Review today's study. Remember that the Holy Spirit is the Paraclete. He is always with you.

What will you do today to recognize the presence of the Holy Spirit?

_____

List the problems, decisions, feelings, and goals you need to discuss with Him today.

_____

Now write a prayer covering this list with the Holy Spirit. Spend time listening to Him as well as talking to Him.

_____

Write down this week's passage to memorize.

_____

SPIRITUAL TRUTHS

- The Holy Spirit is with me always.

- I can talk to the Holy Spirit about everything.

- He counsels and guides me whenever I ask.

Day 5: THE SPIRIT LEADS IN ALL TRUTH

INTRODUCTION

Jesus promised, "You will know the truth, and the truth will set you free" (John 8:32). So how do we know the truth?

At times, even when we have right motives and the best intentions, we deceive ourselves and others. We believe we know the truth even when we don't. One evening as I was leading our small group Bible study, I affirmed, "There is nothing we can do to please God." What I meant was that we cannot earn God's saving grace. But that's not what I said. People in the group questioned me, but I held fast to my error. My stubbornness silenced the questions, but it didn't silence the Holy Spirit.

Later that evening the Spirit awakened me and began to deal with my pride as a teacher and my unwillingness to learn and receive from others. Then the Holy Spirit took me to God's Word and showed me all the things that please God. I was particularly convicted by Romans 14:8, 18; 1 Corinthians 7:32; 2 Corinthians 5:9, 15; Galatians 1:10; 6:8; Colossians 1:10; and Hebrews 11:6. We live to please Him because we love Him, not to earn what He freely gives us.

Although my friends could not convince me of the truth during the Bible study, the Holy Spirit could and did teach me the truth. He leads us in all truth!

EXPLORE THE WORD

Are You Listening to His Teaching?

The Holy Spirit desires to continually teach you all truth. He helps you discern between truth and myth. Often religious myths will control your life and keep you from experiencing the fullness of the Spirit. Only truth can set you free to walk fully in the Spirit.

📖 **Write your own definitions of *myth* and *truth*.**

A myth is _____

Truth is _____

Let me suggest to you that a myth is something that is experienced as truth by some people, some of the time, in some situations. As a result, that experiential, situational "truth" is elevated to the level of absolute truth. But truth is never situational or conditional.

God's truth is unconditional. His absolute truth is true for all people, all of the time, in all situations: "Every good gift and every perfect gift is from above, and comes down from the Father of lights, with whom there is no variation or shadow of turning. Of His own will He brought us forth by the word of truth, that we might be a kind of firstfruits of His creatures" (James 1:17–18 NKJV).

The Holy Spirit takes the truth of God's Word and teaches it to us in every place, for every person, every situation, and every time.

📖 **Read the following verses and summarize what Jesus teaches about the Holy Spirit.**

John 14:17:

_____

John 15:26:

_____

John 16:13:

_____

The Spirit of truth teaches you all truth. He dwells in you, giving you a hunger for God's Word, which is always true.

📖 **Read Psalm 19:7–11. List all the ways that God's words, laws, precepts, and commands are true and perfect.**

_____

EXAMINE YOURSELF

Are You an Eager Student of the Spirit?

The delight of every teacher is a zealous, eager-to-learn student. The same holds true for the Holy Spirit. He delights in your zeal for God's Word. The Holy Spirit has much to teach you. He wants to hide and seal God's Word in your heart so that you will not sin.

How does the Spirit teach you?

- He gives you a hunger and thirst for God's Word by leading you into all truth—God's Word (John 14:17).

- As the Spirit teaches you truth, the Word is being hidden in your heart so that you will not sin against God (Ps. 119:11).

- How can you know that sin lurks in your heart (Ps. 19:12–14)? Out of your heart your mouth will speak (Matt. 12:34). If God's Word has been taught and hidden in your heart by the Spirit, then you will not sin. Rather, you will speak His Word. But if you have deposited in your heart what is not of the Spirit, then you will speak hurtful and sinful things.

Do you long to please God with both the words of your mouth and the meditation of your heart? If so, let the Holy Spirit create in you a zeal, hunger, and thirst for God's Word. Then drink in all the truth and feed on the bread from heaven because all Scripture is inspired by the Spirit to teach you (2 Tim. 3:16).

Pray this prayer aloud and often today and in the coming days:

> *May the words of my mouth and the thoughts of my heart*
> *be pleasing to you,*
> *O LORD, my rock and my redeemer. Amen. (Ps. 19:14)*

EXPERIENCE THE HOLY SPIRIT

When Will You Enter the Spirit's Classroom?

To learn, you must be taught. Paul gave us this insight: "Yet faith comes from listening to this message of good news—the Good News about Christ" (Rom. 10:17). Are you listening to the Spirit? Are you allowing Him to teach you?

Check the ways you are in the Spirit's classroom being taught the truth of His Word:

☐ Daily reading, studying, and meditating on His Word.

☐ Regularly studying His Word with other believers with a teacher in a small group or a class.

☐ Hearing God's Word preached and proclaimed in worship.

☐ Listening to God's Word taught on radio, TV, and tapes, through seminars, retreats, and so forth.

☐ Listening to and singing God's words in psalms, hymns, and spiritual songs. You may be listening to and singing in a live setting or with tapes and CD's.

☐ Memorizing God's Word.

☐ Reading books that teach the truths from God's Word.

☐ Other: _____

The more you hunger and thirst for His Word, the more you will experience the presence and teaching of the Holy Spirit.

MY DAILY WALK IN THE SPIRIT

📖 **Review what you have learned and experienced in the Spirit today.**

Describe how the Holy Spirit is teaching you the truth of God's Word today.

_____

What truths have you most recently learned?

_____

What will increase your zeal and hunger for the Spirit's teaching?

_____

Write a prayer asking God to fill you with the Spirit's hunger and thirst for truth.

_____

Write what this week's passage to memorize means to you.

_____

SPIRITUAL TRUTHS

- The Holy Spirit teaches me and leads me in all truth.
- The Spirit of truth will fill me with hunger and thirst for God's Word.
- When I seek out the Spirit's classroom, I will experience the Spirit's teaching.

Week 3

THE SPIRIT ACTS

The book of Acts in the New Testament chronicles the birth of the church at pentecost and how the early Christians experienced the Holy Spirit. Their experience of the Holy Spirit is both defining and exemplary of how we experience the Holy Spirit today.

Jesus promised His disciples that He would baptize them with the power of the Holy Spirit so that they could boldly witness to the gospel from Jerusalem into the whole world:

> Do not leave Jerusalem until the Father sends you what he promised. Remember, I have told you about this before. John baptized with water, but in just a few days you will be baptized with the Holy Spirit . . . But when the Holy Spirit has come upon you, you will receive power and will tell people about me everywhere—in Jerusalem, throughout Judea, in Samaria, and to the ends of the earth. (ACTS 1:4–5, 8)

Are you ready to experience the power of the Holy Spirit? This week you will discover how through the power of the Holy Spirit, people were saved, healed, delivered, and transformed into bold witnesses in the book of Acts. You may say, "I've never experienced anything like what happened in the book of Acts in my life or church." Nonetheless, you can experience the Holy Spirit in power today.

A friend in ministry remarked to me, "I don't believe in signs and wonders today. They were only for the early church. All of the miracles, healings, signs, and wonders ceased at the end of the apostolic age." I was puzzled by his remarks. Why would God empower the early Christians and then leave us powerless? Why would the God who healed and performed miracles in the Old Testament, the ministry of Jesus, and the early church suddenly stop healing and doing miracles? His nature never changes, so why would His actions change? Why would the Holy Spirit give gifts in the New Testament to believers and not give them to believers today?

The truth is that the Holy Spirit today empowers your life and the church just as He did in the book of Acts. The acts of the Holy Spirit recorded in that book are normative for us today. As you experience the Holy Spirit this week, you will discover how the Holy Spirit desires to empower your life and use you as a Spirit-filled vessel to proclaim the good news with signs and wonders.

Consider Jesus' promises for you:

> The truth is, anyone who believes in me will do the same works I have done, and even greater works, because I am going to be with the Father. You can ask for anything in my name, and I will do it, because the work of the Son brings glory to the Father. Yes, ask anything in my name, and I will do it! (JOHN 14:12–14)

> Go into all the world and preach the Good News to everyone, everywhere. Anyone who believes and is baptized will be saved. But anyone who refuses to believe will be condemned. These signs will accompany those who believe: They will cast out demons in my name, and they will speak new languages. They will be able to handle snakes with safety, and if they drink anything poisonous, it won't hurt them. They will be able to place their hands on the sick and heal them. (MARK 16:15–18)

> "Yes," he told them, "I saw Satan falling from heaven as a flash of lightning! And I have given you authority over all the power of the enemy, and you can walk among snakes and scorpions and crush them. Nothing will injure you. But don't rejoice just because evil spirits obey you; rejoice because your names are registered as citizens of heaven." (LUKE 10:18–20)

When you experience the Holy Spirit, you will see God do mighty things in you and through your life to glorify the name of Jesus. When was the last time you prayed for people who were sick and saw them healed by the power of the Holy Spirit? When did you boldly witness that Jesus is Savior and Lord? When did you see the Holy Spirit perform miracles? In the book of Acts, the early Christians saw the Holy Spirit at work all around them, and daily they went to the temple praising God. Get ready. Their experience will become your experience of the Holy Spirit.

This Week's Passage to Memorize

> When the Holy Spirit has come upon you, you will receive power and will tell people about me everywhere—in Jerusalem, throughout Judea, in Samaria, and to the ends of the earth. (ACTS 1:8)

Day 1: THE SPIRIT'S POWER POURED OUT

INTRODUCTION

Not everyone is ready for the Spirit's power. Not then, in the first century; not now, today. Have you ever wondered what happened to all the early believers who witnessed the resurrection of Jesus? More than five hundred saw the risen Christ. Paul wrote,

> I passed on to you what was most important and what had also been passed on to me—that Christ died for our sins, just as the Scriptures said. He was buried, and he was raised from the dead on the third day, as the Scriptures said. He was seen by Peter and then by the twelve apostles. After that, he was seen by more than five hundred of his followers at one time, most of whom are still alive, though some have died by now. Then he was seen by James and later by all the apostles. Last of all, I saw him, too, long after the others, as though I had been born at the wrong time. (1 COR. 15:3–8)

Where were all those who saw Him risen on the day of pentecost? Only about 120 believers remained in Jerusalem waiting for the baptism of the Holy Spirit. Jesus had promised that if they waited, they would be baptized with the Holy Spirit. What could have kept the other 380 witnesses away? Perhaps what kept them away has kept you away from the fiery baptism of power in the Holy Spirit.

 Check any reasons or excuses you have had for not experiencing the baptism of the Holy Spirit:

☐ Too busy with life's demands and responsibilities

☐ Afraid of losing control

☐   Don't know how to be baptized by the Spirit

☐   Not ready for the experience

☐   Not interested

☐   Other: _____

What happens when the Holy Spirit baptizes believers with power? Let's find out.

EXPLORE THE WORD

What Happened to the Early Believers?

We read in Acts 2 that on the day of pentecost, the 120 believers who had remained in Jerusalem were meeting together when suddenly the Holy Spirit blew through the room they were in like a wind. That shouldn't surprise you. You have already studied how the breath and wind of God in the Old Testament were the Holy Spirit.

God's wind, the Holy Spirit, blew through the room, and tongues of fire rested above the heads of the believers. Everyone present was filled with the Holy Spirit and began speaking in other languages or tongues. As they poured out onto the streets, those in Jerusalem were amazed that they could understand the words of Peter and the believers, no matter what their native tongue happened to be. Some of the bystanders thought that the believers were drunk. But Peter explained what had happened.

 Read Acts 2:14–21. Describe how Peter explained the manifestation of the power of the Holy Spirit.

_____

After the Holy Spirit baptized the early believers, those believers witnessed the power of the Holy Spirit in many ways. Those demonstrations of power are available today to all believers.

 Read Acts 2–3. List all the mighty acts that God's Spirit accomplished when His power was released.

_____

_____

(Check your list against mine: people are saved, become generous, share the Lord's Supper, speak in unknown tongues, pray with power, do signs and wonders, fear God, get their needs met, boldly witness, become joyful, praise God, meet often together for worship, see miracles.)

Now go back to your list, and circle all the acts of the Spirit that you see in your personal life or your church.

EXAMINE YOURSELF

What's Happening in My Life?

Based on what happened at pentecost, how would you evaluate the work of the Holy Spirit in your life? The Greek word translated "power" in Acts 1:8 is *dunamis*. It means the wonder-working power of God. How is the Spirit's *dunamis* at work in your life?

Powerless Christianity is the symptom of the Spiritless life. A life baptized by the Holy Spirit is filled with wonder-working power from God. Is your life filled with the demonstrations of His powerful presence?

Complete the following sentences:

I worship and praise God _____

I boldly witness to Christ when _____

I see signs and wonders _____

I see people saved _____

I experience powerful prayer _____

I give _____

I witness miracles and healings _____

I speak in unknown tongues _____

I experience the Spirit's power _____

If you had a hard time completing these sentences, then you may not be experiencing the Spirit's power in your life as the early Christians did. Don't be discouraged. You can ask in prayer for the Spirit's baptism and filling of power.

EXPERIENCE THE HOLY SPIRIT

Do You Want the Baptism of the Holy Spirit?

Jesus baptizes His followers in the Holy Spirit. His baptism comes in power. Paul wrote, "I have won them over by the miracles done through me as signs from God—all by the power of God's Spirit" (Rom. 15:19). Are you ready to win others to Christ by the power of the Holy Spirit?

Pray for the baptism of the Holy Spirit:

> *Lord Jesus, I ask You to baptize me with the Holy Spirit. Fill me with the Spirit's power so that I may experience and demonstrate Your power in all the ways the early Christians experienced the baptism of the Spirit. I pray that the signs and wonders done through me will glorify Jesus and bring many lost people to salvation in Him. Amen.*

Lewis Sperry Chafer commented,

> The spiritual life is not passive. Too often it may look that way when we speak of ceasing from ourselves and our own efforts. The point is that we need to learn to live and serve by the power God has provided, not self-effort. A true spiritual life is even more active, enlarged and vital because the limitless power of God energizes us . . . Spirit-filled Christians are quite likely to feel physical exhaustion at the close of the day the same as other people. They are weary *in* the work, but not weary *of* the work.

Not long ago I almost took our vacuum cleaner to the repair shop. I couldn't get it to run even after taking it apart, cleaning it, and examining it thoroughly. Then I noticed a crimp in the cord and discovered that a wire in the power cord was severed. Without power, the vacuum would never run, no matter how clean it was. No matter how clean your life is, without power—from the baptism of the Holy Spirit—you will be powerless to experience the miracle-working power of the Holy Spirit. Plug into the Spirit's power today.

MY DAILY WALK IN THE SPIRIT

Review what you have learned and experienced in the Spirit today.

Demonstrations of a life baptized by the Spirit include the following:

_____

One way my life is filled with the Spirit's power is

_____

Right now, I am not seeing in my life certain things that the Spirit-filled early believers saw in their lives. Those missing manifestations of His power include the following:

_____

The signs and wonders I am seeing as the Spirit is at work around and in me are

_____

Write a prayer thanking Jesus for baptizing you with the Holy Spirit.

_____

Write this week's passage to memorize.

_____

SPIRITUAL TRUTHS

- Jesus promised to baptize me with the Holy Spirit.

- When the Holy Spirit comes upon and fills me, His power is demonstrated.

- I will see the same signs and wonders, miracles, healings, and other demonstrations of power as the early church saw.

Day 2: POWER TO SAVE

INTRODUCTION

When the Holy Spirit baptizes us with His power, people all around us get saved. Recently I was teaching on the family to a group in Malaysia. Approximately four hundred people had gathered from churches throughout the area. I assumed that they were all Christians—born again and saved by the Lord Jesus Christ.

As I began to share on God's plan for marriage and the family, the Holy Spirit prompted me to stop and share the gospel. Obedient to the Spirit, I shared that we could never hope to have healthy, prosperous marriages and families unless everyone in the family was saved and then completely sold out and obedient to Jesus Christ. I shared the basic gospel message and remarked that some of those who were there were just going through the religious motions of faith but did not have a personal relationship with Jesus Christ.

I gave an altar call, and more than forty people stood up and accepted Jesus Christ. Religious people may appear to have life together, but unless they are born of the Spirit, they cannot live the Christian life filled with the Holy Spirit.

EXPLORE THE WORD

Are People Around You Getting Saved?

When the Holy Spirit baptized those early believers, thousands around them were saved. The baptism of the Spirit brought powerful boldness to their witness. They were not afraid to tell everyone that God had raised Jesus from the dead—not even the Jewish leaders who had crucified Jesus. They didn't fear persecution, imprisonment, or even death. The Holy Spirit had transformed a group of frightened, hiding followers of Jesus into dynamic witnesses of faith who turned the world upside down (Acts 17:6).

Read each scripture, and then summarize what the Holy Spirit did through the newly emboldened believers.

Acts 2:41–42:

_____

Acts 2:47:

_____

Acts 4:4:

_____

Acts 4:32–35:

_____

Acts 5:12–16:

_____

Acts 6:7:

_____

The baptism and filling of the Holy Spirit empower us to witness boldly to the saving power of Jesus Christ.

EXAMINE YOURSELF

Does Anything Keep You from Being a Bold Witness?

The Holy Spirit's power is available to you to give you the words to say even when others are skeptical or critical of Jesus. Jesus promised that the Spirit would give you the words you need to be a bold witness.

Read **Mark 13:11** and **Luke 12:11–12.** Complete the sentences at the top of the next page.

The most difficult setting for me to share Christ is _____

The one thing that keeps me from sharing Jesus is _____

These basic issues keep us from sharing Jesus:

- Fear of being ridiculed, rejected, or persecuted

- Ignorance about what to say

- Shame about how we have lived our lives

The Holy Spirit conquers our spirit of fear with power (2 Tim. 1:7). He puts the words in our mouths that we need to share (Mark 13:11; Luke 12:11–12), and He takes away all shame due to condemnation (Rom. 8:1–2).

EXPERIENCE THE HOLY SPIRIT

Will You Boldly Witness?

Peter and the other early church leaders and believers were persecuted on every side. Yet they boldly witnessed. The Holy Spirit empowered them to suffer every kind of emotional and physical abuse so that the gospel would be spread throughout the world. Peter preached, "We are witnesses of these things and so is the Holy Spirit, who is given by God to those who obey him" (Acts 5:32). We read that those early believers "preached God's message with boldness" (Acts 4:31).

Over the years in speaking to youth, my friend Ken Davis has made three important points. As Christians, we have (1) nothing to fear, (2) nothing to lose, and (3) nothing to hide.

Complete these sentences:

The one thing I fear the most is _____

The one natural thing I could never lose is _____

The one thing I must hide is _____

More than three hundred times in Scripture, God says to us in one form or another, "Fear not." One preacher commented that God tells us not to fear more than 365 times in Scripture because we need to hear His encouragement daily. When I think of my fears, I fear most losing any of my family members to hell. I would be overwhelmingly grieved to lose in death any of my dear loved ones. And at times, I feel I must hide my mistakes and failures. What about you? Our great fears have been defeated—Jesus conquered sin and death. Jesus promised that whatever we lose for His sake will be abundantly returned to us. And He promised to bring whatever is hidden in the dark into the light.

Those early Christians literally stared fear in the face, lost everything material, and often sacrificed their lives. They hid nothing but exposed everything for the sake of the gospel.

📖 Read Hebrews 11:33–40.

The Holy Spirit will empower you to face anything, even death itself, to share the gospel of Jesus Christ. I was on a platform in Baroda, India, with evangelist Peter Youngren when a Hindu mob of radical fundamentalists attacked the crusade. They threw rocks and fire-bombs into the crowd and at us on the platform. I thought, *You know, we could die here*. Yet I and all those on the platform felt an overwhelming sense of peace and calm. We knew we were doing God's will, and the Holy Spirit calmed and comforted us even in those dire circumstances.

Do you desire to experience the Holy Spirit? Share the gospel daily with all you meet. Every word you share, if you let Him, will be given to you by the Spirit. Every moment you share will be an encounter with the power and presence of the Spirit of God!

MY DAILY WALK IN THE SPIRIT

Review what you have learned and experienced in the Holy Spirit today.

What I need to overcome through the Spirit's power daily in order to witness boldly is

_____

One person I know I need to witness boldly to is _____

I will witness to this person (identify a day or an occasion) _____

_____

Write a prayer surrendering to Christ whatever you fear, whatever you possess, and whatever is hidden in your life.

_____

Write down this week's passage to memorize.

_____

SPIRITUAL TRUTHS

- The Holy Spirit will give me the boldness I need to proclaim the gospel.

- In the power of the Spirit, I have nothing to fear, lose, or hide.

- When I ask Him, the Holy Spirit will give me just the right words about Jesus to say to the lost.

Day 3: Power for Signs and Wonders

Introduction

I had rarely seen any signs and wonders in my twenty years of ministry. Then one night I found myself sitting in a miracle service hosted by one of the well-known healing evangelists of our time. With power and boldness he preached the gospel, and thousands were saved. Then he led the large crowd there in worship as we prepared to see God do miracles. Suddenly throughout the large stadium, hundreds began to stream forward to praise God for their healings.

Some stood up from wheelchairs and walked for the first time in years or in a lifetime. People who were blind saw; people who were deaf heard. At the name of Jesus, scores of people received miracles. Since then, I have witnessed many different signs and wonders. Some were financial miracles. Others were supernatural signs that pointed to the presence of God in our midst. The Holy Spirit is at work all around us to point people to Jesus and bring glory to God the Father.

Explore the Word

What Signs and Wonders Did the Holy Spirit Demonstrate?

The power of the Holy Spirit flowed freely through the early church. Believers and skeptics alike were awestruck with the fear of God by the working of His mighty power. The sick were healed, the dead were raised, the lost were saved, and the oppressed were delivered.

Read each scripture listed at the top of the next page, and write a brief description of the signs and wonders noted there.

Acts 2:22: _____

Acts 2:43: _____

Acts 4:29–30: _____

Acts 5:12: _____

Acts 6:8: _____

Acts 8:6: _____

Acts 8:13: _____

Acts 14:3: _____

Acts 15:12: _____

The Holy Spirit acted with signs and wonders to lead the lost to Christ and to confirm the truth of the gospel.

EXAMINE YOURSELF

What Signs and Wonders Are You Witnessing?

Those who never expect God's Spirit to move miraculously rarely see miracles. Faith in God's power to act in our midst opens our eyes to a multitude of signs and wonders. Without faith, we cannot see. Jesus said,

> "For the hearts of these people are hardened,
>   and their ears cannot hear,
>   and they have closed their eyes—
> so their eyes cannot see,
>   and their ears cannot hear,
>   and their hearts cannot understand,
> and they cannot turn to me
>   and let me heal them."
> But blessed are your eyes, because they see; and your
> ears, because they hear. (MATT. 13:15–16)

Because of the lack of faith among the people, very few miracles were wrought at the hands of Jesus in Nazareth (Matt. 13:58).

Are few miracles worked by the Spirit around you because of a lack of faith? Or is your life overflowing with signs and wonders because you allow the Spirit to do as He pleases with and through you?

📖 **List the greatest hindrances in your life to signs and wonders.**

_____

📖 **People getting saved is the most awesome miracle.** Next to that, describe a sign or wonder you have witnessed in your life.

_____

EXPERIENCE THE HOLY SPIRIT

Have You Asked Lately?

One reason we fail to see the Holy Spirit perform signs and wonders in our lives is that we fail to ask. James observed, "And yet the reason you don't have what you want is that you don't ask God for it" (James 4:2).

Do you want signs and wonders to follow you (Mark 16:17)? Then pray for God to send His Spirit in power, as the early believers prayed.

📖 **Pray this prayer adapted from Acts 4:29–30:**

And now, O Lord, hear the threats of my enemies, and give me, Your servant, great boldness in my preaching and sharing the gospel. Send Your healing power; may miraculous signs and wonders be done through the name of Your holy servant Jesus. Amen.

By faith in Jesus, you will see the Holy Spirit move around you with signs and wonders.

MY DAILY WALK IN THE SPIRIT

Review what you have learned and experienced in the Spirit.

I experience a lack of signs and wonders in my life because

_____

The greatest signs and wonders at the hand of the Spirit that I witness are

_____

I am believing God for a miracle

_____

Write a prayer asking God to send His Spirit in power in your life and your church so that mighty signs and wonders to His glory will happen.

_____

Write this week's passage to memorize.

_____

SPIRITUAL TRUTHS

- Signs and wonders will follow me as I trust the power of the Spirit to work in and around me.

- Signs and wonders happen in the Spirit's power when the name of Jesus is lifted up and God receives glory.

- I have the privilege to pray for people to be saved and signs and wonders to be manifested for His name's sake.

Day 4: POWER FOR PRAYER

INTRODUCTION

I have prayed with literally thousands of people at the altar, in homes, airports, hospitals, cars, planes, and scores of other places. I have seen people saved, healed, and delivered through the power of God's Spirit. I know that my prayers do not save, heal, or deliver—Jesus does! I also recognize that the power to pray and the knowledge of what to pray come from the Holy Spirit.

> When you are at a loss for what to pray—ask the Holy Spirit!
> When you don't know for whom to pray—ask the Holy Spirit!
> When words fail you—ask the Holy Spirit to intercede through you!
> When you are hopeless, helpless, and harried—ask the Holy Spirit!
> When you are lost and need to be found—ask the Holy Spirit!

EXPLORE THE WORD

When Do You Pray?

When should we pray? The simple answer is: *all the time*. Paul urged, "Pray at all times and on every occasion in the power of the Holy Spirit" (Eph. 6:18). When the persecution became intense, the early believers prayed. The way they prayed can model for us the way to pray in the power of the Spirit.

Read the prayer at the top of the next page. Underline all the phrases that you can pray right now for the situations you face.

O Sovereign Lord, Creator of heaven and earth, the sea, and everything in them—you spoke long ago by the Holy Spirit through our ancestor King David, your servant, saying,

"Why did the nations rage?
    Why did the people waste their time with futile plans?
The kings of the earth prepared for battle;
    the rulers gathered together
against the Lord
    and against his Messiah."

That is what has happened here in this city! For Herod Antipas, Pontius Pilate the governor, the Gentiles, and the people of Israel were all united against Jesus, your holy servant, whom you anointed. In fact, everything they did occurred according to your eternal will and plan. And now, O Lord, hear their threats, and give your servants great boldness in their preaching. Send your healing power; may miraculous signs and wonders be done through the name of your holy servant Jesus. (ACTS 4:24–30)

Now read Acts 4:31–37. Describe all the ways the early believers lived out their faith and walked by the power of the Spirit.

_____

_____

_____

EXAMINE YOURSELF

How Is Your Power Prayer Life?

Praying in the Spirit is praying in power! You may pray in your own language or your prayer language (1 Cor. 14:13–17) or with groans and tears. You may pray eloquently or simply, loudly or silently. You may pray sitting, standing, walking, bowing, kneeling, or lying prostrate. You may pray with hands lifted up or hands folded reverently. The key to power prayer is not your language, position, or sounds. Power prayer is always in the Spirit: "You, dear friends, must continue to build your lives on the foundation of your holy faith. And continue to pray as you are directed by the Holy Spirit" (Jude 20).

Take time to pray. Take five minutes or more, and read Romans 8:26–27. Now invite the Holy Spirit to pray through you. He will give you the words you need. He will bring to mind the people and situations you need to pray for. He will guide your prayers. After you have let Him pray through you, describe what happened.

_____

_____

_____

When the Spirit prays through you, God's will in heaven is prayed on earth, and spiritual power is released to bring His kingdom on earth as Jesus taught us to pray: "Thy kingdom come. Thy will be done in earth, as it is in heaven" (Matt. 6:10 KJV).

EXPERIENCE THE HOLY SPIRIT

Ask for Power to Pray

The Holy Spirit will empower you to pray. But you have to ask Him. You cannot develop your prayer life through listening to others pray or reading the prayers of others. However, you can invite the Holy Spirit to give you prayer power.

I invite you to pray something like this:

Holy Spirit, at times I feel powerless when I pray. But I know that all the power I need to pray resides in You. I ask You to empower me to pray for the right things in Your perfect time and will so that what You desire to be accomplished in me might happen right now. By Your power transform me into a mighty prayer warrior in God's kingdom. Amen.

MY DAILY WALK IN THE SPIRIT

Review what you have learned and experienced in the Spirit.

My prayers are most effective when

_____

My prayers are least effective when

_____

List the ways the Spirit prays through you.

_____

Write a prayer inviting the Holy Spirit to pray through you without ceasing.

_____

Write this week's passage to memorize.

_____

SPIRITUAL TRUTHS

- The Holy Spirit empowers me to pray.

- The Holy Spirit will help me pray even when I don't know how or what to pray.

- When I pray in the Spirit, God's kingdom and will come on earth.

Day 5: Power for Healing

INTRODUCTION

Throughout the book of Acts, the Holy Spirit acted to heal. God is the One who heals. He healed throughout the Old Testament and the ministry of Jesus. And His healing power flowed through the early church.

Healing has a particular purpose—to give glory to God. Healing is not about the one being healed. It's about the Healer! Healing flows from the Father, through the Son, and is effected by the power of the Holy Spirit.

Jesus' ministry was characterized by preaching the kingdom of God, saving the lost, healing the sick, and delivering people from demonic oppression. The Holy Spirit continues that ministry through His body today, the church. The Holy Spirit gifts believers to heal.

📖 **Read 1 Corinthians 12:6–9.**

EXPLORE THE WORD

Does God Heal?

The healing power of God can be witnessed through Scripture. God the Healer (*Jehovah Ropha*) performs miracles of healing by His Spirit throughout history. Asking someone, "Do you believe in healing?" is a moot question. Whether or not we believe that God heals doesn't alter the truth—God heals.

📖 **Read each passage at the top of the next page, and write down what you learn about how God heals.**

Genesis 20:17: _____

Exodus 15:26: _____

Deuteronomy 32:39: _____

2 Chronicles 7:14: _____

Psalms 30:2; 103:3; 107:20: _____

Isaiah 53:5: _____

Jeremiah 17:14: _____

Matthew 4:23: _____

Matthew 14:14: _____

Mark 6:56: _____

Luke 5:17: _____

John 5:1–15: _____

Acts 3:1–9: _____

That God heals is not a matter of speculation. It is truth.

EXAMINE YOURSELF

Do You Believe That God Heals You?

God can and will heal, whether or not you believe it. The point here is simple: Do you believe that God heals you? Jesus said to the woman with an issue of blood, "Daughter, your faith has made you well. Go in peace. You have been healed" (Mark 5:34).

Do you have the faith in God to allow the Spirit's healing power to flow in you and through you to others?

Read Acts 3:1–11 and answer these questions:

How would you have responded to the beggar's request?

_____

When someone today asks you to pray for his healing, how do you respond?

_____

The oil of God's Spirit is available through faithful prayer for healing:

 Read James 5:14–16.

Experience the Holy Spirit

Will You Pray for the Sick?

The early church prayed, "Send your healing power; may miraculous signs and wonders be done through the name of your holy servant Jesus" (Acts 4:30). You will not experience the Spirit's power to heal without faith and prayer.

 List those who are sick for whom you will pray.

_____

 Write a prayer asking God to send His healing power for the people on your list.

_____

Pray specifically. Pray in faith. Pray in the Spirit. Pray for people who are sick to be healed and also saved and delivered from any oppression.

Have you ever wondered how many remain sick because we as believers fail to pray?

My Daily Walk in the Spirit

📖 **Review what you have learned and experienced in the Spirit.**

When I pray for the sick, I

_____

The most awesome physical healing miracle I have witnessed is

_____

I need the Spirit to teach me in praying for the sick how to

_____

Write a prayer asking the Lord to remove all hindrances to your praying in faith and power for the sick to be healed.

_____

Write this week's passage to memorize, and describe what it means to you.

_____

Spiritual Truths

- God heals.

- The Holy Spirit can empower me to pray for the sick to be healed.

- I need to pray for the Healer to save, heal, and deliver others.

Week 4

THE SPIRIT'S GIFTS AND FRUIT

When Jesus gave us the Spirit, He baptized us with the power to serve others in His name and to be like Him. Paul wrote, "All who have been united with Christ in baptism have been made like him" (Gal. 3:27). In Galatians 5:22–23 the fruit of the Spirit are listed:

> When the Holy Spirit controls our lives, he will produce this kind of fruit in us: love, joy, peace, patience, kindness, goodness, faithfulness, gentleness, and self-control.

The fruit of the Holy Spirit are the nature and character dwelling within us so that we might be like Jesus.

Have you ever tried even for a day to be like Jesus in your own strength? As a child, I would try very hard to be good for a whole week, especially if I wanted a special privilege from my parents, such as a new toy or a trip to the fairgrounds. My goodness train usually derailed during the first day. I would say or do something that shattered every illusion I had of self-made perfection. All too often I rediscovered the truth that Jeremiah knew: "The human heart is most deceitful and desperately wicked. Who really knows how bad it is? But I know! I, the LORD, search all hearts and examine secret motives. I give all people their due rewards, according to what their actions deserve" (Jer. 17:9–10).

The fruit of the Spirit equal the nature of Christ. As I matured in my spiritual walk, I discovered that Christ living in and through me by the Spirit was the only way I could reflect His nature. The deposit of the Spirit in the soil of my heart bears the fruit of the Spirit:

- Love—having unconditional love of the Father that seeks to love even the unlovely.

- Joy—feeling joy from within that is not affected by external situations and circumstances.

- Peace—ceasing of enmity with God and others.

- Patience—waiting on God's will, in God's way, within God's timing and for God's glory.

- Kindness—seeking God's best to be demonstrated through me for others.

- Goodness—having both pure motives and actions.

- Faithfulness—always trusting God and being trustworthy.

- Gentleness—preferring others to myself.

- Self-control—taking responsibility for my thoughts, actions, feelings, and attitudes; completely surrendering myself to the Lord.

Paul indicated that as Spirit-filled believers, we have this assurance: "For this is the secret: Christ lives in you, and this is your assurance that you will share in his glory" (Col. 1:27). His nature abides in us by the power of the Spirit.

The gifts of the Spirit equal the ministry of Christ. How does the nature of Jesus work in and through us to touch the lives of others? By the Spirit's empowering us through His gifts to do the ministry of Jesus in the world.

Read 1 Peter 4:10–11.

Answer the following questions:

How are you experiencing the nature of Christ at work in your life today?

_____

_____

What ministry is Christ doing through you today?

_____

_____

This week you will be discovering how the nature and ministry of Christ live in you and work through you by the Holy Spirit's power. For you to experience the Spirit's empowering fruit and gifts in your life, you must live a yielded life, completely abandoned to His lordship. Paul declared, "The Spirit Himself bears witness with our spirit" (Rom. 8:16 NKJV). In reflecting on this verse, Oswald Chambers wrote,

> Why doesn't God reveal Himself to you? He cannot. It is not that He will not, but He cannot, because you are in the way as long as you won't abandon yourself to Him in total surrender. Yet once you do, immediately God witnesses to Himself—He cannot witness to you, but He instantly witnesses to His own nature in you. If you received the witness of the Spirit before the reality and truth that comes from obedience, it would simply result in sentimental emotion. But when you act on the basis of redemption, and stop the disrespectfulness of debating with God, He immediately gives His witness. As soon as you abandon your own reasoning and arguing, God witnesses to what He has done, and you are amazed at your total disrespect in having kept Him waiting.
> (*My Utmost for His Highest*, October 22)

Are you ready for God to reveal the witness of His Spirit through the nature and ministry of Christ in your life? Then prepare to surrender all so that His gifts and nature might flow through you as you experience the Holy Spirit this week.

This Week's Passage to Memorize

> There are different kinds of spiritual gifts, but it is the same Holy Spirit who is the source of them all. There are different kinds of service in the church, but it is the same Lord we are serving. There are different ways God works in our lives, but it is the same God who does the work through all of us. A spiritual gift is given to each of us as a means of helping the entire church.
> (1 COR. 12:4–7)

Day 1: The Spiritual Fruit of Love, Joy, Peace, and Patience

INTRODUCTION

Each one of these fruit could fill days, weeks, and months of our study. Our focus in the next two days will be on how these fruit are reflected in our lives. Fruit begins with a seed. Unless something is sowed, there is no harvest. Even when a seed is sowed, care and attention have to be given to that seed for it to bear good fruit.

The Holy Spirit uses only one kind of seed for producing the nature of Christ in our lives. That seed is the Word of God. Jesus teaches that the seed in our lives is the Word of God.

Read Mark 4:1–20. Describe the kind of soil in your heart.

_____

What are you doing to care for the seed in your heart?

_____

What keeps the seed from growing in your life?

_____

Once God's Word has been sown into the soil of our hearts, the Holy Spirit cultivates that seed. He uses that seed to convict, guide, correct, comfort, and teach us. As we respond to His work in us (called sanctification), we grow spiritually and begin to bear fruit in our lives. That fruit serves, ministers to, and blesses the lives of others so that they will begin to hunger after His Word and desire spiritual fruit in their lives.

EXPLORE THE WORD

What Are the Fruit in You?

Each of the fruit of the Spirit is listed here. You can know what each fruit looks like by reading Scripture and, in particular, by examining the life of Jesus. His life manifested each fruit of the Spirit.

Read the passages about each of the fruit, and write down how that passage describes or defines that fruit.

Love

1 Corinthians 13: _____

John 13:34–35: _____

1 John 4:7–13: _____

Luke 10:25–28: _____

Joy

Nehemiah 8:10: _____

Psalm 28:6–7: _____

Isaiah 61:3: _____

John 16:20–24: _____

Philippians 4:4–7: _____

Peace

Romans 5:1–2: _____

John 14:27; 16:33 _____

Romans 14:17: _____

2 Corinthians 13:11: _____

Patience

Isaiah 40:31: _____

Romans 12:12: _____

Romans 5:3–5: _____

1 Corinthians 4:12–13: _____

Love always seeks God's best for the other person. Joy always springs from the rejoicing within us because we are redeemed. Peace always brings reconciliation between us and God and between us and others. Patience always waits and acts in God's perfect timing and will.

EXAMINE YOURSELF

Are His Fruit Growing in You?

How are these fruit growing in your life? Self-examination doesn't bring a greater determination to do better or try harder. Rather, growing in the Spirit's fruit requires greater surrender and abandonment on our parts. The negative and sinful attitudes and habits within us behave like weeds that choke out the Spirit's fruit.

Read Mark 7:14–23 and Galatians 5:16–21. List the weeds that need to be pulled from the soil of your life so that His fruit may grow unimpeded.

_____

Put yourself on the line. Put an X where you are right now in regard to each of the following fruit.

Loving	Indifferent	Hateful
Joyful	Passive	Sad
Peaceful	Uneasy	In Conflict and Turmoil
Patient	Restless	Impatient

What will the Holy Spirit need to do in you to help you move more toward the left in these continuums? What are the areas of your strongest resistance to the Spirit?

_____

EXPERIENCE THE HOLY SPIRIT

Are You Letting His Fruit Manifest?

Over the years, I have observed that people hungering after the Holy Spirit often seemed more concerned with the operation of the gifts in the church than with the ongoing manifestation of His fruit. If the gifts operate without the fruit, then ministry becomes manipulative, controlling, intimidating, and legalistic. Without the fruit of the Spirit, gifts are talents operating in human power and effort to use others. Zechariah warned, "It is not by force nor by strength, but by my Spirit, says the LORD Almighty" (Zech. 4:6).

Christ's nature in you must control the gifts flowing from you in service. Perhaps you have been looking for some goose-bumps experience of the Spirit. Yes, at times you may experience the Holy Spirit's tangible touch of power, warmth, and awe in your life. But a steadfast walk in the Spirit manifests His fruit in an ongoing, daily way.

Do you desire to experience the Spirit? Complete these sentences:

I will share God's love with _____ today by _____

I will share God's joy today with _____ by_____

I will make peace with _____ today by _____

I will be patient with _____ today by waiting on God to _____

Pray this prayer as you grow in His fruit:

Lord Jesus, cultivate the fruit of Your Spirit in my life so that I may be more like You. Teach me to love the unlovely, to rejoice even in trials and suffering, to be at peace with others, and to be patient as You use me in Your plan, according to Your will for Your glory. Amen.

My Daily Walk in the Spirit

Review today's study. Ask God's Spirit to use the Word to grow the fruit of love, joy, peace, and patience in your life.

The fruit of the Spirit that needs the most unrestricted release and growth in my life is:

   ☐ love   ☐ peace   ☐ joy   ☐ patience

Write a prayer asking the Lord to remove the hindrances and grow that fruit.

_____

The fruit of the Spirit that I am seeing the most progress in is

   ☐ love   ☐ peace   ☐ joy   ☐ patience

The area of my life that I am most reluctant to totally surrender is _____

_____

Surrender that area in prayer now. Write your prayer of surrender.

_____

Write the passage to memorize for this week.

_____

Spiritual Truths

- The Spirit's fruit are grown in my heart's soil prepared by surrender and obedience.

- Abandonment is a key to my spiritual growth.

- Without the fruit of the Spirit, gifts are never more than talents used to manipulate and control others.

Day 2: THE SPIRIT'S FRUIT OF KINDNESS, GOODNESS, FAITHFULNESS, GENTLENESS, AND SELF-CONTROL

INTRODUCTION

Years ago I sat in a counseling training session with the prolific and noted pastoral counselor Wayne Oates. One of the participants asked, "What advice would you give us to share with husbands and wives having marital difficulties?" Dr. Oates simply quoted the apostle Paul, "Be kind to one another." Has kindness permeated your walk in the Spirit?

Kindness involves preferring others to ourselves. Paul wrote, "Don't be selfish; don't live to make a good impression on others. Be humble, thinking of others as better than yourself. Don't think only about your own affairs, but be interested in others, too, and what they are doing" (Phil. 2:3–4). The antidote to selfishness and pride is kindness and gentleness. Who has benefited today from a special act of kindness from you?

Goodness is impossible in our own strength. Jesus made it plain that no one is good except God (Matt. 19:17). The only good in us is the good imparted to us by the indwelling Holy Spirit. As He makes us holy (sanctifies us), the goodness of Christ saturates us body and soul.

Faithfulness asks, Where do your loyalties lie? In other words, have you placed trust in God or man? Faithfulness also implies a steady stability to stay on course and stand firm in the midst of every attack. Paul asserted, "My dear brothers and sisters, be strong and steady, always enthusiastic about the Lord's work, for you know that nothing you do for the Lord is ever useless" (1 Cor. 15:58). Now that defines faithfulness.

Gentleness seeks God's best for the other person. Rudeness puts self ahead of another person's interests, but gentleness speaks truth in love and tries to minister God's kindness to others.

Self-control points us to being directed by the Holy Spirit instead of our own desires, wants, and lusts of the flesh. Are you in control of areas in your life? Now is the time to give it up. Surrender control to the Spirit.

EXPLORE THE WORD

Are You Like Jesus?

Much has been written about defining moments in life. Your conversion and baptism were defining moments. How you handled certain major crises in your life defined your character and integrity. Getting married and having children are defining moments.

📖 **What about you?** Describe two or three major defining moments in your life.

_____

📖 **More important than our defining moments are the defining people in our lives.** Write down the names of some of the people who were influential in leading you to Jesus Christ or in helping you grow spiritually as a young Christian. Then write a brief prayer of thanksgiving for them.

_____

_____

The key defining person in our lives is Jesus Christ. His character and nature define who we are, how we think and behave, and what we do. These five fruit of the Spirit help to define his character in us. Describe each fruit based on the passages next to it.

Kindness (Ps. 116:5–9; Eph. 4:32; Col. 1:10): _____

Goodness (Ps. 25:8–9; Rom. 7:4; 2 Cor. 9:10): _____

Faithfulness (Josh. 23:7–8; Pss. 15; 57:2–3; 89:8; James 4:5–7):_____

Gentleness (Ps. 18:35; Col. 3:12; 1 Tim. 6:11):_____

Self-control (2 Tim. 1:7; Titus 2:12; 1 Peter 1:13): _____

EXAMINE YOURSELF

Where Do You Manifest These Fruit?

These five fruit of the Spirit should be manifested in every area of our lives. However, we may hinder their growth in certain areas. When we take control, we stifle the fruit of the Spirit. When He is in control, His fruit grow abundantly in every area of life.

Complete these sentences:

The area in my life where I lack kindness is _____

The area in my life that needs more goodness is _____

The area in my life where I'm less than faithful to the Lord is _____

The area in my life where I tend not to be gentle is _____

The area in my life that needs more self-control is _____

As you examine these fruit in your life, think of the results you see when these fruit manifest themselves. Complete these thoughts:

I see the kindness of God toward me in _____

When I am kind, I notice that _____

I experience God's goodness most in _____

God's faithfulness to me is _____

I experience the gentleness of God most when _____

When I am self-controlled, the benefit is _____

EXPERIENCE THE HOLY SPIRIT

So Where Are You Growing?

Growing in the Spirit means that you are dying to the old self and living anew in Christ. His Spirit is more evidenced in your life through your relationships, at home, work, church, and leisure. You rarely experience instant spiritual growth in any area of life. Experiencing the fruit of the Spirit in your life is never as much about what you do as what you release or allow the Spirit to do.

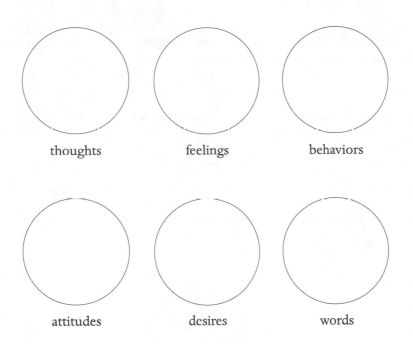

On each circle shade in the area of sanctification—the Spirit's holiness and fruit—in that area. For example, if at least half of the time, your thoughts are sanctified by the Spirit, then shade the "thoughts" circle in 50 percent. Do this for each of the six areas.

thoughts   feelings   behaviors

attitudes   desires   words

For the unshaded areas, write a prayer repenting of the things in that area of your life that hinder the Spirit and asking the Holy Spirit to sanctify and take full control.

_____

MY DAILY WALK IN THE SPIRIT

Review today's study. Your life will demonstrate the nature of Christ as the Spirit's gifts mature in you.

What is the Holy Spirit convicting you about in regard to the gifts of kindness, goodness, faithfulness, gentleness, and self-control?

_____

Name a person to whom you find it difficult to be kind, and write a prayer asking God's Spirit to empower you with that fruit.

_____

Write a prayer asking God's Spirit to help you develop more self-control in

_____

Write the passage to memorize for the week.

_____

SPIRITUAL TRUTHS

- The fruit of the Spirit reflect the character of Christ in my life.

- As the Spirit sanctifies areas of my life, I will reflect more of Christ to others.

- Only the Spirit has the power to grow and mature fruit in my life. As I submit to Him, I become more like Christ.

Day 3: POWER GIFTS

INTRODUCTION

In the body of Christ, His church, many different spiritual gifts are given for the purpose of helping the church: "Now there are different kinds of spiritual gifts, but it is the same Holy Spirit who is the source of them all. There are different kinds of service in the church, but it is the same Lord we are serving. There are different ways God works in our lives, but it is the same God who does the work through all of us. A spiritual gift is given to each of us as a means of helping the entire church" (1 Cor. 12:4–7).

We had a need in one of our children's Sunday school classes for another teacher on our teaching team. A woman in our church was known to be an excellent elementary teacher in the public schools. So the Sunday school coordinator for the elementary classes and I visited with her about joining the team. "Oh, I couldn't do that," she responded. Not satisfied with "no" as an answer, I probed deeper.

"Is your schedule too full to teach, or by Sunday are you simply too tired of teaching children all week that you can't do it again?" I asked.

"None of the above," she remarked. "I teach math and science at school. I have a talent to teach, but I'm simply not gifted in teaching children at church. What I love doing is visiting the hospital and shut-ins. Is there a place in those ministries that I can serve?" she inquired.

The Holy Spirit taught me something important in that conversation. Natural talent does not necessarily equate spiritual gifting. A spiritual gift (*charisma*) is imparted to you by the Holy Spirit to empower you to minister to others in the body of Christ. While the Holy Spirit may use a natural talent you have in ministry, you may not necessarily have natural skills for your gifts. But you will receive supernatural power from the Spirit to minister in the gift(s) He gives you.

EXPLORE THE WORD

What Are the Spirit's Gifts?

For the purpose of this study, I have categorized the spiritual gifts listed in the New Testament into three categories—power gifts, body gifts, and ministry gifts. The first set of spiritual gifts we will explore is found in 1 Corinthians 12.

 Read 1 Corinthians 12. Now list the nine gifts of the Spirit mentioned in this chapter.

1._____

2._____

3._____

4._____

5._____

6._____

7._____

8._____

9._____

 Review 1 Corinthians 12. Describe the reasons the Spirit gifts believers.

_____

_____

 Write down Paul's instructions in 1 Corinthians 12 and 14 for the proper use of power gifts.

_____

_____

EXAMINE YOURSELF

What Gifts Have You Been Given?

The gift of *wisdom* is the Spirit's gift to apply God's Word, His wisdom, to life situations in profitable, timely, and unique ways. Gifted with wisdom, the believer is able to understand and practically use God's Word for himself and speak it to others.

 I have ministered to others with this gift.

I have been ministered to by this gift.

I need the Holy Spirit to give me a deeper understanding of this gift.

The gift of *knowledge* is the Spirit's gift to discern particular knowledge about another person and to apply God's Word in knowing that person's situation. For example, the Holy Spirit may reveal to you that another person is hurting in a relationship with a child and give you an encouraging or comforting word from Scripture for that person.

 I have ministered to others with this gift.

I have been ministered to by this gift.

I need the Holy Spirit to give me a deeper understanding of this gift.

The gift of *faith* is the Spirit's gift to believe and trust God supernaturally for Him to provide and move in situations to accomplish His will. The Spirit gives extraordinary confidence to a believer to trust God for His plan in specific circumstances even when others may not have that intensity of faith.

 I have ministered to others with this gift.

 I have been ministered to by this gift.

 I need the Holy Spirit to give me a deeper understanding of this gift.

The gift of *healing* is given by the Spirit to minister God's power to heal to the physically and emotionally hurting in the body of Christ. Praying for the sick to be healed is part of a believer's privilege and responsibility.

I have ministered to others with this gift.

 I have been ministered to by this gift.

 I need the Holy Spirit to give me a deeper understanding of this gift.

The gift of *the working of miracles* is the Spirit's gift to allow the Spirit to do supernatural signs and wonders through a believer's life. These miracles both bless believers and point unbelievers to Jesus, the Miracle Worker.

☐ I have ministered to others with this gift.

☐ I have been ministered to by this gift.

☐ I need the Holy Spirit to give me a deeper understanding of this gift.

The gift of *prophecy* given by the Spirit empowers a believer to speak boldly the word of the Lord to the body or a person. This gift is forthtelling God's word as well as foretelling His plan and will. The Holy Spirit reveals what the Father wants to say (John 16:13–15). Any prophetic word that a believer receives needs to be tested by the Word of God, confirmed by the witness in the believer of the Holy Spirit, and also confirmed in the testimony of other believers. Prophetic words are to be helpful, encouraging, and comforting (1 Cor. 14:3).

☐ I have ministered to others with this gift.

☐ I have been ministered to by this gift.

☐ I need the Holy Spirit to give me a deeper understanding of this gift.

The gift of *discerning of spirits* is given by the Holy Spirit to help a believer know and understand when evil or demonic spirits are influencing, oppressing, or attacking others. Part of that discernment is the ability to discern the confession of a person who truly believes in Jesus as Lord and Savior (1 John 4:1–4).

☐ I have ministered to others with this gift.

☐ I have been ministered to by this gift.

☐ I need the Holy Spirit to give me a deeper understanding of this gift.

The gifts of *speaking in tongues* and *interpretation of tongues* are given by the Holy Spirit to empower a believer to share the gospel in other languages (Acts 2), to pray in the Spirit (1 Cor. 14:14), and to speak prophetically by the Spirit (1 Cor. 14:1–13). The interpretation of tongues is given by the Spirit so that those who hear tongues may understand what the Spirit has said.

☐ I have ministered to others with these gifts.

☐ I have been ministered to by these gifts.

☐ I need the Holy Spirit to give me a deeper understanding of these gifts.

EXPERIENCE THE HOLY SPIRIT

Are You Ministering with His Gifts?

The purpose of power gifts is to minister to and help other believers. You will experience the power of the Holy Spirit to minister in these gifts as you step out in faith to help another person in need. For example, the Holy Spirit may lead you to pray for someone who is sick. The gift of healing will be stirred within you to minister to that person. You are not the healer; Jesus is. But He can touch someone with His healing power through the gift of healing operating in and through you.

When the Holy Spirit prompts you to minister with a power gift, how do you respond?

Circle any of the feelings that represent your response:

- Bold
- Fearful
- Compassionate
- Reluctant
- Unsure
- Confident
- Uneasy

- Hesitant
- Expectant
- Hopeful
- Enthusiastic
- Doubting
- Filled with the Spirit
- Other: _____

The Holy Spirit needs willing vessels through whom to minister His grace and power. He has gifted you to be a minister and operate in the gifts. Being gifted by the Spirit is not about your ability but about your availability to be used by Him. Are you available?

My Daily Walk in the Spirit

Review today's study. Let the Holy Spirit stir up His gifts in you to minister to others.

Describe a time when you were ministered to by one of the power gifts you studied today.

_____

Describe a time when you ministered to another person with a power gift and what the Spirit did in you and him.

_____

Write a prayer asking God's Spirit to use you to minister to others with His gifts.

_____

Write down this week's passage to memorize.

_____

Spiritual Truths

- The Holy Spirit has gifted me to minister to others.

- To be used by the Spirit in gifted ministry to others, I must be willing and available.

- I can receive ministry from other believers through the Spirit's gifts.

Day 4: Body Gifts from the Spirit

Introduction

In addition to the spiritual gifts listed in 1 Corinthians 12, the apostles Paul and Peter wrote about many more body gifts. These gifts help the body do ministry within the body and to the outside world. Although Scripture lists some twenty-seven gifts from the Spirit, we might conclude that since the Spirit is infinite, so are His gifts. He continually gifts and empowers people for ministry.

For example, one gift not formally designated as such in Scripture is that of intercession. Intercessory prayer, praying for others, is mentioned often in the Bible but never labeled as a gift of the Spirit. However, we know that the Spirit intercedes and prays through us when we don't know how to pray (Rom. 8:26). You may not be able to find the name for the spiritual gift at work in you on a list, but you know that God is using you in ministry. Don't limit the Holy Spirit. Let Him work in you to stir up the gifts within so that others might receive ministry.

In labeling the gifts we are studying about today as body gifts, we are referring to them as ministry gifts given by the Spirit operating in the church. They are just as Spirit filled and empowered as the gifts we studied yesterday.

Explore the Word

What Gifts Are at Work in and Through You?

Paul compared the church to a body and affirmed that every member of the body is important and necessary to the whole. You have an important ministry in the body of Christ. It is no more or less important than other ministries. Every gifting is necessary for the whole body or church to function properly.

Read Romans 12:6–8. List the body gifts mentioned in this passage.

_____

_____

Read 1 Peter 4:10–11. List the gifts mentioned in this passage.

_____

_____

Review the lists of body gifts you have made. Underline all the gifts that are operating in your church. Circle the gifts that are in you or that have touched your life.

EXAMINE YOURSELF

How Is the Spirit Ministering Through You?

In Romans 12:7 Paul wrote, "If your gift is that of serving others, serve them well." In many ways, all the gifts point to this truth: we are to serve one another. The purpose of the body gifts is to serve, not to be proud about them or to point attention at an individual. Jesus commands us to be servants.

Body gifts used by servants build up the lives of others. Christ's hands, feet, touch, and voice are yours. His ministry to the body flows through believers.

What ministry is the Holy Spirit gifting you to do right now? Describe how He is speaking to you to use your gifts in the body.

_____

EXPERIENCE THE HOLY SPIRIT

Are You Praising God for the Gifts in Others?

A mutuality exists among believers in ministering to and serving one another. Listen to Paul: "If one part suffers, all the parts suffer with it, and if one part is honored, all the parts are glad. Now all of you together are Christ's body, and each one of you is a separate and necessary part of it" (1 Cor. 12:26–27). So if you need ministry, someone has been gifted in the body to minister to your need. And someone is waiting for the spiritual gifts in you to minister to him.

Never envy the gifts in others. They are there to bless you and others in the body. Never become proud of your gifts. You don't own or possess them. The Holy Spirit has given you those gifts not for others to praise you but for you to serve them.

Write a prayer praising and thanking God for the body gifts that have ministered to you and your church.

_____

_____

My Daily Walk in the Spirit

Review today's study. Ask the Holy Spirit to reveal to you the gifts operating through you for body ministry.

Think over the last year and describe the gifts the Lord has used through you for ministry.

_____

Think of some of the people active in ministry in your church. Write down their names and the gifts in them for ministry. Then pray over the list, thanking God for using them.

_____

Look over the lists of body gifts you have made today. Are any of them not operating in your church? If so, write them down, and then pray for the Spirit to stir up those gifts in your church for ministry.

_____

Write the passage to memorize for this week.

_____

Spiritual Truths

- The Holy Spirit has gifted me with body gifts to serve others in the church.

- When I am ministered to through body gifts, I need to praise God.

- I seek spiritual gifts to serve others, not to receive praise for myself.

Day 5: The Spirit's Ministry Gifts

Introduction

First we studied the spiritual gifts listed in 1 Corinthians 12. Then we explored the body gifts listed in Romans 12 and 1 Peter 4. A third listing of gifts can be found in Ephesians 4:11–12. For the sake of our study, we are calling these ministry gifts. Paul told us that Christ gave gifts to the church for ministry. These are often called *office gifts*. These ministry gifts include apostles, prophets, pastors, teachers, and evangelists.

Within a body, the office gifts exist to equip the believers for doing ministry. An evangelist proclaims the gospel to the lost, and he also equips people to evangelize. The pastor pastors and equips people to pastor; the teacher teaches and equips people to teach, and so on.

Apostles are sent forth as missionaries and church planters. Apostles often nurture and equip others for ministry. Prophets forthtell and foretell God's word. Pastors nurture and care for the flock, the sheep. They shepherd the church under the authority of the Good Shepherd, Jesus. Teachers instruct and disciple people in God's Word while evangelists reach out to the lost, seeking to get them saved in Christ Jesus.

Explore the Word

Understanding the Ministry Offices of the Church

Scripture defines the role of each of these offices in equipping the saints. In every congregation, these offices exist to train and disciple people to minister to the saints and reach the world with God's saving power in Jesus.

 Read Ephesians 4:7–14. Then answer the questions on the next page about the equipping ministry gifts of the church.

For what purpose do the ministry gifts exist?

_____

What is the end result of equipping in the lives of believers?

_____

When believers are properly equipped, how will they respond to storms and trials in life?

_____

Read the scriptures describing the following offices, and then describe the function of these offices.

Apostle (Luke 9:1–5; Acts 5:12; 1 Cor. 12:28–31; Eph. 2:20–22):

_____

Prophet (Deut. 18:15–22; 1 Cor. 12:8–11; 14; Eph. 2:20–22):

_____

Pastor (Jer. 23; Titus 1:5–16; James 5:14–15; 1 Peter 5:1–4):

_____

Teacher (Deut. 5:31; Rom. 12:7; 15:14; 1 Cor. 4:15–16; 12:28–31; Col. 1:28; James 3:1):

_____

Evangelist (Matt. 28:18–20; Acts 21:8; Eph. 4:11):

_____

EXAMINE YOURSELF

Have You Been Called to a Ministry Gifting?

God's Spirit calls and ordains specific people for the equipping ministry of the church. These offices are set apart so that believers will be equipped to minister to others. Have you been called to one of these offices by the Spirit's voice?

📖 **Read John 15:16.** Who calls, and how are they called and ordained?

_____

_____

Some are called to make ministry in the church their full-time vocation. Others work outside the church but regard everything they do as ministry. Not all are called to the ministry offices of the church. But those who are called need prayer, encouragement, and support.

📖 **Write a prayer of intercession for one person you know in each of the ministry giftings.**

Apostle:

_____

_____

Prophet:

_____

_____

Pastor:

_____

_____

Teacher:

_____

_____

Evangelist:

_____

_____

EXPERIENCE THE HOLY SPIRIT

Have You Been Called?

If God has called you into full-time ministry by His Spirit, what are you doing with that call? You may also be called to support and pray for a particular person in a specific ministry office. Are you praying? Don't neglect whatever gifts the Spirit has given you for ministry. Paul reminded Timothy, "Do not neglect the spiritual gift you received through the prophecies spoken to you when the elders of the church laid their hands on you. Give your complete attention to these matters. Throw yourself into your tasks so that everyone will see your progress. Keep a close watch on yourself and on your teaching. Stay true to what is right, and God will save you and those who hear you" (1 Tim. 4:14–16).

We are all a body ministering together. Each gifting is essential to the body of Christ for growth and spiritual edification. No matter what your gift is in the body of Christ, you are needed. You are important to the body. No spiritual, body, or ministry gift in the body is optional or unnecessary. Use your gifts. Fulfill the call of God on your life. Experience the Holy Spirit by yielding to the operation of His gifts in you.

Write a prayer asking the Holy Spirit to empower you with His gifts for ministry.

_____

_____

My Daily Walk in the Spirit

 Review today's study. Ask the Holy Spirit to impart His gifts to you that He desires you to use in the body for ministry.

Read 1 Corinthians 14:1, then list the spiritual gifts that you desire for ministry.

_____

Write a prayer asking the Holy Spirit to give you these gifts to fulfill God's purpose and plan for you.

_____

Begin interceding for your church that all of these gifts would be stirred up in the body of Christ where you worship and minister. Write down how the Spirit tells you to intercede.

_____

Recalling the passage to memorize for the week, describe what it means to you after this week's study.

_____

Spiritual Truths

- The Holy Spirit may call and ordain me to a ministry office in the body.

- I need to pray for those in the ministry offices in the body of Christ.

- I should not neglect the gift that is in me for ministry.

Part 2

Experience the Spirit's Presence

Week 5

THE SPIRIT'S INDWELLING PRESENCE

How could Jesus promise, "Be sure of this: I am with you always, even to the end of the age" (Matt. 28:20)? He has ascended to heaven and sits on the right hand of God. Yet Jesus also promised, "Yes, I am the vine; you are the branches. Those who remain in me, and I in them, will produce much fruit. For apart from me you can do nothing" (John 15:5). Beyond all that, Jesus exclaimed, "For my flesh is the true food, and my blood is the true drink. All who eat my flesh and drink my blood remain in me, and I in them. I live by the power of the living Father who sent me; in the same way, those who partake of me will live because of me" (John 6:55–57).

Abiding with Christ or Christ indwelling us remains shrouded in mystery unless we understand the indwelling presence of the Holy Spirit. Jesus lives in us through the Holy Spirit. This week we will discover that the Holy Spirit has taken up residence in our lives. In fact, our bodies are His temple, and our hearts tabernacle the presence of God's Spirit within us.

Read each of the following passages, and describe where the Spirit of God lives.

1 Corinthians 3:16–17:

_____

1 Corinthians 6:19–20:

_____

When you die to self (Gal. 2:20–21), the Holy Spirit takes up residence in your life. From that moment forward, the eternal presence of God lives in you and begins to sanctify you—make you holy. Paul affirmed, "It is God's will that you should be sanctified" (1 Thess. 4:3 NIV).

Your life in the Spirit has made a radical change. No longer does your natural identity define *who you are*. Rather, you are now known by *whose you are*. You belong to Christ—body, soul, and spirit. He has bought you with the price of His broken body and shed blood on the cross.

This week you will discover that no matter where you are or where you go, the Holy Spirit indwells your life, transforming your mind into the mind of Christ (Rom. 12:1–2; 1 Cor. 2:16).

This Week's Passage to Memorize

> Or don't you know that your body is the temple of the Holy Spirit, who lives in you and was given to you by God? You do not belong to yourself, for God bought you with a high price. So you must honor God with your body. (1 COR. 6:19–20)

Day 1: Receive the Gift of the Holy Spirit

INTRODUCTION

Have you ever had a gift you didn't open? One year I received a package in the mail a few weeks before Christmas Day. It came before we had the tree up, so I put it in the hall closet close to where we planned to trim the tree. However, I forgot about the present. Christmas Day came and went. I wondered why I had received no present from a certain family member, but that package had slipped my mind. Weeks later as I was cleaning out that closet, the package on the shelf jarred my memory. There sat a gift addressed to me, in my possession, but never opened.

For many Christians, the gift of the Holy Spirit is like that unopened Christmas present. Upon repentance and new birth, we receive the gift of the Holy Spirit (Acts 2:38). But what do we do with God's precious gift? Do we ignore the Holy Spirit and neglect a relationship with Him? Do we fear losing control of our words or actions?

The Holy Spirit both indwells us and abides with us. If He is a silent partner in all that we say or do, then we have failed to receive Him fully into our daily walk. But if we welcome Him into every thought, feeling, attitude, action, and conversation, then He will become for us what Jesus purposed in sending Him to us—our Helper.

EXPLORE THE WORD

Have You Welcomed Him?

Receiving the gift of the Holy Spirit is described in Acts 2:38. Open your Bible and take time to read it carefully.

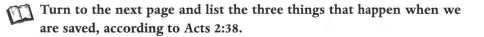 **Turn to the next page and list the three things that happen when we are saved, according to Acts 2:38.**

1. _____

2. _____

3. _____

Let's review what Peter said: "Each of you must turn from your sins and turn to God, and be baptized in the name of Jesus Christ for the forgiveness of your sins. Then you will receive the gift of the Holy Spirit" (Acts 2:38). Turning away from our sins is called *repentance*. When we confess Jesus Christ as Lord and Savior, we obey His command to be baptized (Matt. 28:19). Then we receive the gift of the Holy Spirit.

His indwelling presence resides in every believer. Read the following scriptures, and write down what the Holy Spirit is doing in the life of a new believer.

John 3:1–8: _____

Romans 8:2: _____

Romans 8:14–16: _____

1 Corinthians 12:3: _____

Ephesians 4:4: _____

1 John 5:6–8: _____

Here's the bottom line. The Holy Spirit dwells in you. Have you let Him out? Out into your soul and body. Out into your walk and your talk. Out into your relationships—at home, work, fun activities, and church. Out into everything you say and do.

EXAMINE YOURSELF

So If He's in You, Do You Know Him?

You will come to an intimate knowledge of God through His indwelling Spirit. But the only way that will happen is to welcome and receive the gift of the Spirit within you. Paul stated it bluntly: "Do not stifle the Holy Spirit" (1 Thess. 5:19).

Is anything keeping you from receiving and welcoming the Holy Spirit into every area of your life? At the top of the next page, check any hindrances to the Spirit in you.

☐	Unconfessed sin	☐	Ignorance
☐	Unforgiveness	☐	Lack of desire or hunger for God's presence
☐	Fear of losing control	☐	Unwilling to let go and let God move in my life
☐	Pride	☐	Other: _____

Many Christians I have met try vainly to stay in control of their daily walk. Oh, they've surrendered eternity to Jesus but not today. Some fear losing control of their tongues and speaking in tongues. Some fear losing control of their bodies and doing something embarrassing in front of friends or strangers. After all, that happened to those early Christians. They spoke in tongues and acted like drunkards in front of a whole city. So what?

Surrender complete control to the gift of the Holy Spirit within you. Sin controls whatever He doesn't control in you (Rom. 8:6–11).

EXPERIENCE THE HOLY SPIRIT

Will You Welcome Him?

Have you ever felt like an unwanted guest in another person's home? I have felt that way at times when making an evangelism visit. The unsaved people don't want to appear impolite so they ask you into their house, invite you to sit down, fix you a cup of coffee, and then nervously wait for the right moment to usher you out to the sidewalk. I wonder if we ever treat the Holy Spirit that way?

You can experience His presence in every decision, relationship, and moment of life. The invitation rests in your hands. Welcome and receive the gift of the Holy Spirit.

> **Write a prayer welcoming and receiving the gift of the Holy Spirit into every corner of your body and soul.**

_____

Where the Spirit is welcomed, He comes in power, comfort, counsel, conviction, grace, and guidance.

My Daily Walk in the Spirit

Review today's study. Have you welcomed and received the gift of the Holy Spirit in all of your life?

Describe how you have experienced the indwelling presence of the Holy Spirit in your life.

_____

Confess any areas of your life in which His presence is not welcome, and repent to Him.

_____

Write a prayer thanking God through the name of Jesus Christ for the gift of the Holy Spirit.

_____

Write down this week's passage to memorize.

_____

Spiritual Truths

- As a born-again believer, I have been given the gift of the Holy Spirit.

- I can welcome the Holy Spirit into every aspect of my life.

- Without my invitation, the Spirit cannot visit specific areas of my life with His presence.

Day 2: BORN OF THE SPIRIT

INTRODUCTION

Is there life after birth? The speaker asked the question, which then resonated in my mind and heart. What did he mean? What unsaved humans call life is really just existing. Controlled by the power of sin, we do not really experience life until we meet Life—Jesus Christ. He says to us, "I am the way, the truth, and the life. No one can come to the Father except through me" (John 14:6).

When His life enters us at our conversion, we are born of the Spirit. Born of the flesh, we exist like the First Adam, and our destiny is to die. Born of the Spirit, we become the children of God, and our destiny is eternal life.

EXPLORE THE WORD

Are You Born of the Spirit?

Life is more than existence. Day-to-day existence produces the perfume of death. All we say and do smells of decay. When people smell your life, do they sense death or life in you?

Read this passage, and then paraphrase in your own words how it describes your life before being born of the Spirit.

Once you were dead, doomed forever because of your many sins. You used to live just like the rest of the world, full of sin, obeying Satan, the mighty prince of the power of the air. He is the spirit at work in the hearts of those who refuse to obey God. All of us used to live that way, following the passions and desires of our evil nature. We were born with an evil nature, and we were under God's anger just like everyone else. (EPH. 2:1–3)

_____

_____

Once you left behind existence, you stepped into resurrection power. Paul described it this way: "But God is so rich in mercy, and he loved us so very much, that even while we were dead because of our sins, he gave us life when he raised Christ from the dead. (It is only by God's special favor that you have been saved!) For he raised us from the dead along with Christ, and we are seated with him in the heavenly realms—all because we are one with Christ Jesus" (Eph. 2:4–6). Describe your _life_ after being born of the Spirit.

_____

_____

Read the following scriptures, and describe what it means to be born of the Spirit.

John 1:10–13: _____

John 3:1–8: _____

Romans 8:1–14: _____

EXAMINE YOURSELF

Are You Really Living?

Imagine a baby being born and then staying in an infant developmental state the rest of his life. Never eating meat, drinking only milk, that infant never matured or grew into childhood, adolescence, and finally adulthood. We would say that the immature infant was disabled.

Many Christians love their Spirit-birthed life in a disabled state. They are stuck in infancy. They can tell you how they were born again and what Jesus did for them years ago, but they can't tell you what Jesus did in them today. Where are you in your walk in the Spirit? After being birthed in the Spirit, have you been growing?

Mark an *X* on the line closest to the word that describes where you are right now spiritually.

_____

Infancy   Childhood   Adolescence   Maturity

EXPERIENCE THE HOLY SPIRIT

Are You Ready to Move On?

Too many Christians are stuck in spiritual apathy. Their new birth became mired in mediocrity and routine. Faith turned into religion, and enthusiasm for Jesus turned into ritual. If you are stuck, now is the time to move on from milk to meat in the Spirit.

Read Hebrews 6:1–6. Describe how this passage speaks to your walk in the Spirit today.

_____

_____

No matter what the Spirit has done in your life, there is more. The best is yet to come. You've been called not just to live but also to live life abundantly (John 10:10). Stop looking back, and start looking to Jesus (Heb. 12:1–2).

My Daily Walk in the Spirit

Review today's study. After you were born again, what happened, and what's happening?

Describe when and how you were born of the Spirit.

_____

Write down the major landmarks or defining moments of spiritual growth in your life.

_____

How have you grown in the Spirit? Describe how you are more mature today than you were a year ago.

_____

Write a prayer asking God's Spirit to take you beyond where you are to a new and deeper level of spiritual intimacy with Him.

_____

Write down this week's passage to memorize.

_____

Spiritual Truths

- The only way for me to experience real life was to be born of the Spirit.

- After I was born of the Spirit, God mandated growth and maturity in my life.

- I need to repent of and leave behind whatever keeps me from growing in the Spirit. I look forward to Christ, not backward to the past.

Day 3: ASK FOR THE SPIRIT

INTRODUCTION

I had always thought that the command "Ask and you shall receive" referred to my wants and needs in life. The Holy Spirit is much more than an invisible Santa Claus. He doesn't indwell me to be my sugar daddy! When I got over my spiritual infancy and childlike fantasies, the reality of being indwelt by the Holy Spirit of God hit me.

I needed *of* Him, not *from* Him. As much as a parent showers a child with gifts, no gift means as much as the presence of the parent with the child. As much as the Father is the Giver of every good gift (James 1:17), He desires more of our relationship than supplying my needs. And I need more than just His gifts. I need *the* Gift—I need *Him*.

When I ask for and receive the Spirit in my moment or circumstance, I receive *all* I need. Everything I could possibly want, think, feel, need, or say is *in Him*. When I ask for and receive the presence of the Holy Spirit, I have everything for life.

EXPLORE THE WORD

Are You Asking for the Spirit?

How should we pray? Scripture commands us to pray in the Spirit. To pray in the Spirit, we must first ask for His Spirit to pray in us. The indwelling Spirit prays in and through us (Rom. 8:26). So how must we ask?

Read Luke 11:1–13. Describe how you should pray asking for the Holy Spirit.

Why settle for less in your prayers? Less is asking for needs and wants before asking for the One who has it all—the Holy Spirit. The Spirit knows everything that you need.

Read 1 Corinthians 2. Describe how the Spirit of God intimately knows you.

_____

EXAMINE YOURSELF

When Will You Ask?

Have you ever caught yourself thinking about what you need to pray or planning out your prayer list instead of seizing that moment simply to pray? We spend far too much time thinking about and studying prayer instead of actually *doing it!* Of course, it's beneficial to go to prayer seminars and study about prayer. But actually praying for and receiving the Spirit's presence is needed continuously.

We need His presence to make every decision. In the supermarket, ask Him what to buy and what you should be eating to take care of your body. In the mall, ask Him what you should buy and how to treat the service associates. In church, ask Him how to worship and what to sing. In your family, ask Him what to say to your spouse or children or parents. Consult with the Holy Spirit on every decision. He is the Counselor. Ask Him how to pray.

Take time right now to write a prayer and ask for the Holy Spirit.

_____

EXPERIENCE THE HOLY SPIRIT

What Does He Say?

After you ask for the Holy Spirit, be still. Listen for His voice as you still every other voice in your life. Let Him speak to you when every distraction has been silenced.

Listen. Hear His voice. Be still and know Him. Write down what the Holy Spirit is saying and praying through you.

Asking for the Spirit apart from listening for His voice brings nothing but silence. But asking for the Spirit while listening to His voice brings all that you need.

My Daily Walk in the Spirit

Review today's study. Are you asking for the Spirit?

Write a prayer asking the Holy Spirit to speak to you about every thought, feeling, action, and word in your life today.

_____

List anything that has kept you from asking for the Spirit. Then repent of the things on your list.

_____

Take time to sing and praise the Spirit for all that He has spoken to you. Write down the words to any chorus or song He gives you to sing.

_____

Write down the week's passage to memorize.

_____

Spiritual Truths

- I can and must ask Jesus for the Holy Spirit.

- When I ask *of* Him instead of *from* Him, the Spirit ministers to my every need.

- I must quickly repent of whatever hinders my asking and ask for the Spirit to fill, refresh, and renew me.

Day 4: WALK IN THE SPIRIT

INTRODUCTION

The indwelling presence of the Holy Spirit means that I can walk in the Spirit every moment of life. Walking in the Spirit means that He is in control and leading me. Picture yourself having a partner guiding you around while you are blindfolded. It's called a trust walk. Your spiritual walk is a trust walk. Paul stated, "We walk by faith, not by sight" (2 Cor. 5:7 NKJV).

As you are being led blindfolded by your sighted partner, you must depend on his eyes, not your own; his judgment of where to go and what to avoid, not your own. His strength and knowledge keep you from stumbling and falling. His voice gives direction and guidance to your walk.

EXPLORE THE WORD

What's It Like?

Walking in the Spirit is not a mystical experience where one sees continual visions, dreams dreams, talks in tongues, and performs miracle after miracle. Although signs and wonders follow believers (Mark 16:17), your walk in the Spirit will permeate every aspect of your life, especially the mundane and commonplace.

Read Romans 8 and answer these questions:

What power do sin and the past have over you? _____

_____

How does the Spirit control you? _____

Describe your adoption as a child of God. How are you to act? _____

What is your inheritance? _____

How is the Spirit praying through you? _____

What can separate you from His love? _____

EXAMINE YOURSELF

How Is Your Walk Progressing?

Walking in the Spirit means being a victor, not a victim; a conqueror, not a battle-weary, discarded warrior. Are you walking in victory or defeat? Is your talk about the battle or about the King fighting the battle for you? The indwelling Holy Spirit is greater than anything or anyone you will face in life's trials.

Read 2 Corinthians 10; Ephesians 6:10–20; and 1 John 4:4. Now list the battles you face in the world and what the Spirit has given you to win the battles.

The Battles I Face	The Weapons of the Spirit
_____	_____
_____	_____
_____	_____
_____	_____

EXPERIENCE THE HOLY SPIRIT

Are You Ready?

The indwelling Spirit gives you the power to face anything in life. No trial will be too hard and no temptation too great. Are you ready? Clothed with the armor of God, you have all you need to stand firm in Christ and to go forward in the Spirit.

Never pray for the battles; they will come. Go beyond asking for victory. It has already been won in the cross and resurrection of Jesus Christ. Instead, ask the Holy Spirit to direct each step of your walk. In His leading lies your daily triumph.

This is a fifth-century prayer of the early church. Pray it now.

O Heavenly Father, in whom we live and move and have our being, we humbly pray you so to guide and govern us by your Holy Spirit, that in all the cares and occupations of our daily life we may never forget you, but remember that we are ever walking in our sight; for your own name's sake. Amen. (Venita Wright, ed., *Prayers Across the Centuries* [Wheaton, IL: Harold Shaw Publishers, 1993], 63)

My Daily Walk in the Spirit

Review today's study. Are you walking wounded or victorious?

Confess any area of your walk in which you feel defeat, and ask the Holy Spirit to bring victory in that area.

_____

Describe the one area in your spiritual walk in which you need to develop a deeper level of trust in the Holy Spirit.

_____

Write a prayer inviting the Holy Spirit to walk with you through every decision, conversation, and action you take today.

_____

Write down this week's passage to memorize.

_____

Spiritual Truths

- My walk in the Spirit is victorious because Jesus has already won the battles.

- I can trust the Holy Spirit to control every aspect of my walk of faith.

- I must remember to walk in the Spirit in every detail of the commonplace happenings of life.

Day 5: The Spirit's Indwelling Gives Life

Introduction

The Spirit gives us both abundant life and *everlasting life*. It's impossible for the Spirit to die. Your body may die, but the Spirit in you preserves you so that you are absent from the body and present with the Lord. You are kept until that day when the last trumpet sounds and Jesus returns. Upon His return, the dead in Christ will be raised, the same Spirit that raised Jesus from the dead will give life to your mortal body, and you will be raised from the dead!

Explore the Word

By the Spirit, You Will Live Forever!

The indwelling Holy Spirit guarantees everlasting life for you. He also empowers you to live a life pleasing to Him. Paul warned, "Those who live only to satisfy their own sinful desires will harvest the consequences of decay and death. But those who live to please the Spirit will harvest everlasting life from the Spirit. So don't get tired of doing what is good. Don't get discouraged and give up, for we will reap a harvest of blessing at the appropriate time" (Gal. 6:8–9).

> **Underline the part of the passage in Galatians that fills you with hope and assurance.**

When you become discouraged in your walk, don't focus on what discourages you. Instead, look ahead to the harvest of blessing that Jesus has set before you.

📖 **Read Galatians 6:7.** Describe the good seed your life is sowing as a result of the indwelling Holy Spirit.

_____

EXAMINE YOURSELF

What Are You Sowing?

If you are sowing to the desires of the flesh, then you will reap a harvest of destruction. As you sow in the Spirit, you will reap eternal rewards. The eternal rewards are treasures laid up in heaven. At least three things last forever:

1. **Souls that are saved (Dan. 12:1–4).** List the people the Holy Spirit is helping you tell about Jesus.

_____

2. **Prayers that will burn as sweet incense before the throne of God (Rev. 5:8).** Are you praying in the Spirit without ceasing? Write a prayer inspired in you by the Spirit.

_____

3. **Good works done for His glory to serve "the least of these" (Matt. 25:31–46).** What are you doing to serve others in His name?

_____

EXPERIENCE THE HOLY SPIRIT

Will You Let the Indwelling Spirit Control You?

A Spirit-led life surrenders all control over mind, feelings, attitudes, and actions to the Holy Spirit. You cannot experience the Spirit until _you_ get out of the way. At times, you may be the greatest barrier to someone's acceptance of Jesus. At times, you may be blocking the prayers the Spirit desires to pray through you. At times, you may not be doing the good works He has commanded.

Pray this prayer:

Spirit of God, show me what's in me that keeps You from living through me. Amen.

The Spirit's life in you must flow out of you if others are to ever move from mere existence to real life. Begin today to open up every area of your life to the Spirit's control. God will give you the strength to live a Spirit-led and -controlled life.

Paul wrote to you (put your name in the blank): "I pray that from his glorious, unlimited resources he will give _____ mighty inner strength through his Holy Spirit" (Eph. 3:16).

My Daily Walk in the Spirit

Review today's study. Ask God to fill you with His indwelling Holy Spirit.

Write a prayer thanking God for the harvest of eternal life given to you through the power of His Spirit.

_____

Write down anything that discourages you. Then go back over your list and give each discouragement to the Holy Spirit.

_____

Ask the Holy Spirit in a prayer to reveal anything in you that keeps Him from flowing out of you in witnessing, prayer, and good works.

_____

Write down what this week's passage to memorize means to you.

_____

Spiritual Truths

- Through His power, I can live my life to please the Holy Spirit.

- The Spirit is sowing in and through my life the harvest of everlasting life.

- I need to surrender to His complete control whatever in me blocks the Spirit.

Week 6

THE SPIRIT'S PRESENCE PURIFIES AND MAKES US HOLY

Imagine depositing a drop of a powerful cleaning agent into the midst of a black, oily liquid. Slowly the cleansing drop spreads throughout the filth. Here and there streaks and then lines of clear, clean liquid replace the filth. If you wait long enough, the entire black mess will be saturated by the cleanser and completely transformed into a clean, clear liquid. This word picture provides an analogy of the work of the Holy Spirit in you. The Holy Spirit is making you holy and pure (i.e., sanctifying you).

Deposited into the depth of your spirit is the Holy Spirit (Eph. 1:13–14). Your life in Christ is now a work under construction. The Spirit is cleaning out the filth of sin in your soul and body and making you a new creation (2 Cor. 5:17).

As you welcome the presence of the Holy Spirit into every area of your life, you will discover a cleansing flood of living water refreshing and renewing your thoughts, feelings, attitudes, and actions. This week you will be discovering how wonderfully fresh, pure, clean, and new (i.e., holy) the Holy Spirit is making your spiritual walk. You will also uncover how the Spirit's fiery presence within you set you ablaze with love and zeal for Jesus.

Andrew Murray discussed that fire:

> The fire of God, as it comes to purify, to consume the sacrifice and convert it into its own heavenly light-nature, to baptize with the Holy Ghost and with fire, to transform our being into flames of love,—blessed the man who knows His God as a consuming fire. (*The Holiest of All* [Springdale, PA: Whitaker House, 1996], 515)

This Week's Passage to Memorize

> As for us, we always thank God for you, dear brothers and sisters loved by the Lord. We are thankful that God chose you to be among the first to experience salvation, a salvation that came through the Spirit who makes you holy and by your belief in the truth. (2 THESS. 2:13)

Day 1: THE SPIRIT MAKES US HOLY

INTRODUCTION

The Hebrew word for holy (*qadosh*) means "to be set apart, consecrated, and separated" for the sole use of God Himself. Think about that for a moment. By His Spirit, God is setting you apart for His unique and special purposes. He has consecrated you solely as His. No other person, corporation, or country owns or controls you. Being holy means belonging to and living completely for Christ.

For years as a pastor, I suffered from role confusion. I worked for the church, served the church, pastored the church, and spent hours on end at the church. At some still-undefined point I crossed the line. The church became my mistress. Instead of being the beloved of my Bridegroom, Jesus Christ, I found myself in adultery with the church.

It's seductively easy for a pastor or church leader to follow this path. We confuse what we do in the church with how we relate to the Lord. We are tempted to substitute the church for the Head of the church, Jesus. The Holy Spirit sets you and me as believers apart solely for Him. We are part of the body, the church, but we don't belong to an institution. We belong to Jesus (1 Cor. 3:23).

EXPLORE THE WORD

To Whom Do You Belong?

Being holy means being set apart—belonging solely to Jesus as His bride, His beloved. Later this week we will explore how the Holy Spirit's sanctifying (making us holy) work in us purifies us. Purification is part of being made holy. But now let's turn our attention to being set apart by the Holy Spirit so that we belong solely to Christ.

> **Read each of the passages at the top of the next page, and describe how you belong to Jesus.**

1 Corinthians 3:

_____

Romans 12:4–8:

_____

Romans 8:1:

_____

Romans 1:6:

_____

John 17:10:

_____

John 13:8; 15:21:

_____

The indwelling Holy Spirit is making you holy. One experience you will have of that holiness is the sense that you belong first to Christ and then to those who are also sanctified by the Spirit. Who are they? Other saints (holy ones), of course.

EXAMINE YOURSELF

Lonely or Longing?

When you belong to Christ, you are never lonely. At times, you may be alone with Him, having withdrawn from the world and come apart to pray, commune, and be undistracted in time with Christ.

However, belonging leads to longing. A husband and wife long to be with each other because they love each other. The same is true for parents and children and close friends. Even more so, the indwelling Holy Spirit longs for the One who sent Him, Jesus. The Spirit imparts to you that longing to be with Jesus.

Turn the page and complete the sentences there.

I long to be with Jesus when

_____

My longing to be with Jesus is satisfied by

_____

The Holy Spirit has created a longing in me for

_____

EXPERIENCE THE HOLY SPIRIT

Cry Out for Him

When the Spirit inspires you to long for the Savior, don't hold back. That longing sets you apart for Him. That longing draws you close to Him. That longing creates in you a hunger and thirst for holiness.

Say aloud or pray the following verses from Psalms:

> I waited patiently for the LORD to help me,
>   and he turned to me and heard my cry.
> He lifted me out of the pit of despair,
>   out of the mud and the mire.
> He set my feet on solid ground
>   and steadied me as I walked along.
> He has given me a new song to sing,
>   a hymn of praise to our God.
> Many will see what he has done and be astounded.
>   They will put their trust in the LORD. (Ps. 40:1–3)
>
> O God, listen to my cry!
>   Hear my prayer!
> From the ends of the earth,
>   I will cry to you for help,
>   for my heart is overwhelmed.
> Lead me to the towering rock of safety,

for you are my safe refuge,
    a fortress where my enemies cannot reach me.
Let me live forever in your sanctuary,
    safe beneath the shelter of your wings! (Ps. 61:1–4)

As the deer pants for streams of water,
    so I long for you, O God.
I thirst for God, the living God.
    When can I come and stand before him? (Ps. 42:1–2)

I reach out for you.
    I thirst for you as parched land thirsts for rain.
Come quickly, LORD, and answer me,
    for my depression deepens.
Don't turn away from me,
    or I will die.
Let me hear of your unfailing love to me in the morning,
    for I am trusting you.
Show me where to walk,
    for I have come to you in prayer.
Save me from my enemies, LORD;
    I run to you to hide me.
Teach me to do your will,
    for you are my God.
May your gracious Spirit lead me forward
    on a firm footing. (Ps. 143:6–10)

Set apart by the Holy Spirit, you will long for the One to whom you belong—Jesus.

My Daily Walk in the Spirit

Review today's study. Is your desire for holiness driving you to a deeper hunger and thirst for Him?

In what ways has the Holy Spirit set you apart and separated you from the world?

_____

How has belonging to Jesus created in your spirit a longing for Him?

_____

Write a prayer thanking the Lord for giving you His Spirit, who makes you holy.

_____

Write this week's passage to memorize.

_____

Spiritual Truths

- The Holy Spirit has set me apart and is making me holy unto the Lord.

- Set apart and holy, I belong solely to Jesus.

- Because I belong to Him, I continually long and thirst for Him.

Day 2: BAPTIZED BY FIRE

INTRODUCTION

The only way we can be made holy is to be purified by the Spirit's baptism of fire.

📖 **Read Matthew 3:11–12.**

The Holy Spirit cleanses us by fire. He burns away everything in us that is unholy, unclean, and impure. As trials and tests arise in our lives, we experience the fiery presence of the Holy Spirit refining our faith as pure gold.

EXPLORE THE WORD

Refined by the Spirit's Fire

When the Holy Spirit leads you through trials and tests, your trust turns solely to Jesus. All idols—money, success, power, sensuality, and pride—are destroyed by His fire. His fiery love and jealousy consume whatever you were depending on other than Jesus.

📖 **Read 1 Peter 1:6–8 and then answer these questions:**

What must you endure?

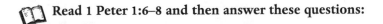

_____

_____

What is the purpose of fiery trials?

_____

_____

What is your response to be?

_____

_____

The fiery trials you experience produce the fruit of holiness in you. What is this holiness? Read the following scriptures, and write down how they describe holiness.

Leviticus 11:44–45:

_____

1 Thessalonians 4:3–8; 5:23:

_____

Hebrews 10:10:

_____

1 Peter 2:8–9:

_____

The Spirit's fiery baptism in your life burns away the chaff of the world and deepens your trust in Jesus.

EXAMINE YOURSELF

Ask the Holy Spirit to Baptize You in Fire

Why would anyone desire such a baptism by fire? Because without it, we cannot be pure and holy. Until we're squeezed, we'll never know what will come out. Until the pressure is on, we'll not know how we will respond under pressure. The fire reveals what's in our hearts. The fire burns away self, making room for the Spirit to create in us a new heart.

The Holy Spirit will not tolerate sin. Where filth is, He will not abide. Thus, the Spirit and sin cannot occupy the same place. Whenever He comes in contact with sin in your life, He will burn it away.

Are you willing to pray David's prayer for cleansing? If so, pray Psalm 51 aloud.

EXPERIENCE THE HOLY SPIRIT

Prepare for His Fire

When you invite the Holy Spirit to baptize you with fire, don't be surprised when the sin in your life is exposed. How will He expose it? You will be convicted by a message, scripture, or comment made by another believer. You will hear yourself say things that embarrass the Holy Spirit *and you*. You will become aware of feelings and attitudes that cause you to weep before the Lord in repentance. Fiery baptism often brings the tears of repentance.

Do not withdraw from the flame of His love. Let the fire consume you. Sin will be purged. What remains will be a fiery passion for Jesus. You will experience the Holy Spirit as you passionately love Jesus.

Invite the Spirit's baptism of fire. Read Hebrews 12:28–29 and Jeremiah 6:29. Write down what you know the Spirit's fire needs to consume and refine in your life.

_____

Whatever the Spirit's fire consumes, that place now purified becomes holy and consecrated unto Him.

MY DAILY WALK IN THE SPIRIT

Review today's study. Let the Holy Spirit's fire burn in your soul and body, consuming all that is not holy.

List and surrender the idols in your life to the Spirit's fire.

_____

Identify any place in your body or soul that isn't consecrated to His Spirit, and invite the Spirit to make it holy.

_____

Write a prayer inviting the Spirit's fire to consume you with a passionate love for Jesus.

_____

Write down this week's passage to memorize.

_____

SPIRITUAL TRUTHS

- I need the baptism of the Spirit's fire to burn away all the chaff in my life.

- Every place He purges with fire becomes a holy place consecrated unto God.

- The Spirit's fire burns within me as a passionate love for Jesus.

Day 3: PURIFIED BY THE SPIRIT

INTRODUCTION

When the Spirit sanctifies us (makes us holy), He makes us pure. To be holy also means to be pure and clean. The apostle Peter told us, "God the Father chose you long ago, and the Spirit has made you holy. As a result, you have obeyed Jesus Christ and are cleansed by his blood" (1 Peter 1:2).

The Holy Spirit purifies us in many ways. First of all, He cleanses us of all immorality and keeps us morally pure. Next, the Spirit cleanses our thoughts and attitudes so that we have pure motives. He gives us a pure heart. By applying the blood of Jesus to our lives, the Spirit cleanses us of sin and wickedness.

EXPLORE THE WORD

Spiritual Purity

Only the pure in heart see God: "God blesses those whose hearts are pure, for they will see God" (Matt. 5:8). We cannot make ourselves pure. But the Spirit cleanses our inner selves and washes us as white as snow.

Discover what the Bible says about purity. Read each scripture, and write down all the qualities of purity described within it.

Psalm 18:24–28: _____

Psalm 24:4: _____

Psalm 51:1–2, 7:_____

Psalm 119:9: _____

Proverbs 15:26: _____

Proverbs 16:1–2: _____

Luke 11:34: _____

2 Corinthians 7:1: _____

Hebrews 9:14; 10:22: _____

James 3:17: _____

As the Spirit makes us holy, our lives are made pure in God's sight by the blood of Jesus.

EXAMINE YOURSELF

Are You Pure?

Every area of life needs the cleansing purification of the Spirit.

Check the areas of your life that need to be cleansed.

☐ TV shows	☐ Motives
☐ Movies and videos	☐ Attitudes
☐ Music	☐ Desires
☐ Internet surfing	☐ Relationships
☐ Language	☐ Sexual behavior
☐ Thoughts	☐ Other: _____

To stay pure requires a constant accountability to God's Word and other Christians who will confront you with the truth in love when you evidence impurity in your life.

In *Discipline and Discovery,* Albert E. Day writes,

> Let us remind ourselves that the purity we seek can never be our own achievement. There is a strange paradox here—only the pure in heart shall see God;

only those who see God shall be pure in heart. No disciplines, none proposed here nor elsewhere, can make us pure. But, it is equally true, without self-discipline there can be no divine deliverance.

. . . For the attainment of that lower purity, from the indulgence of the flesh:

— Read no books and see no pictures which inflame desire . . .

— Indulge in no stories nor listen to any that have an unclean sex-reference . . .

— Avoid anything which lowers your inhibitions . . .

— Set a watch at the door of your eyes. Lusting often begins with looking.

— Guard your imagination. In a contest between the will and imagination, the imagination usually wins . . .

— Do not run into temptation. Some associations are corrupting.

— Restrain your indulgent curiosity . . .

— Let your thoughts dwell on what to do and be rather than on what to avoid or shun.

— Especially keep your mind occupied with Christ and the pattern he has given you.

(Quoted in *Disciplines for the Inner Life* by Bob and Michael W. Benson [Waco, TX: Word, 1985], 246–54)

In the quotation by Albert Day, underline the two or three steps you need to take to focus on purity in your life.

EXPERIENCE THE HOLY SPIRIT

Will You Let Him Purify You?

The Holy Spirit will not use an unclean vessel. "But," you protest, "what about immoral evangelists who lead people to Jesus?" Be assured that the power to minister comes through the Spirit's anointing on God's Word, which never returns void. The impure vessels are convicted, judged, and put through the fire by the Holy Spirit. One may hide sin for a season, but sin will always find the person out (Num. 32:23).

Write a prayer asking the Holy Spirit to purify every area of your life and convict you of any hidden sin.

_____

The Holy Spirit not only purifies; He helps keep you pure.

Pray this aloud for purity:

O God our judge and savior, set before us the vision of your purity and let us see our sins in the light of your countenance; pierce our self-contentment with the shafts of your burning love and let that love consume in us all that hinders us from perfect service of your cause; for as your holiness is our judgment, so are your wounds our salvation. Amen. (William Temple, quoted in *Prayers Across the Centuries*, 137)

My Daily Walk in the Spirit

Review today's study. Ask the Holy Spirit to deal with any impurity that arose in your life today.

What did you learn about God's demand for purity in your life?

_____

What process does the Holy Spirit use in your life to convict you of impurity and cleanse you?

_____

To whom are you accountable in staying pure in your walk?

_____

Write a prayer asking the Holy Spirit to keep you pure.

_____

Write down this week's passage to memorize.

_____

Spiritual Truths

- The Holy Spirit insists that I become and stay pure.

- Staying a pure vessel, I can be used powerfully by the Spirit.

- Being accountable to another believer can help me stay pure.

Day 4: Following the Spirit's Leading in Everything

Introduction

If we are to walk in holiness, then the Spirit must lead us in every part of our lives. Paul wrote, "If we are living now by the Holy Spirit, let us follow the Holy Spirit's leading in every part of our lives" (Gal. 5:25). We Christians may be tempted to segment or compartmentalize our lives. Each compartment is separate from and unrelated to the others. Church is separated from home, and home from work, and leisure from church, and so forth.

Have you compartmentalized the Holy Spirit into the spiritual compartments of your life and refused to let Him lead you in other areas? He insists on holiness in every area of life, not just your religious and spiritual compartments.

The world often accuses us of being hypocrites. We act one way at church and another way in business or at home. Such duplicity betrays the fact that the Holy Spirit is not being allowed to lead us in every part of life.

Explore the Word

Is the Spirit Leading in Everything?

Holiness doesn't pertain only to church or spiritual matters. If holiness doesn't permeate the way that we treat our families or our colleagues at work, then there is no point in claiming to follow Jesus.

📖 **Read Galatians 5:25, and then paraphrase it in your own words.**

_____

We may believe that the Spirit is leading us in our prayer lives but not in our financial giving. Or we may let the Spirit control our sexual morality but not our tongues, and so we gossip. Gossips may believe they are morally superior to fornicators, but they are also sinning against the Spirit. Let's look at a biblical example.

Ananias and Sapphira thought they could appear to worship God and be generous givers in the church while hiding some of their financial arrangements from both God and other believers. They thought wrong!

📖 **Read Acts 5:1–11.** Answer the following questions:

What parts of their lives did Ananias and Sapphira try to control without the leading of the Holy Spirit?

_____

What happened to them as a result of lying to the Holy Spirit?

_____

Do you think that hypocrisy is the equivalent of lying to the Holy Spirit?

_____

EXAMINE YOURSELF

Are You Deceiving Yourself?

Believing that we are led by the Spirit while still keeping control of certain parts of our lives is self-deception. We may be in the process of surrendering control of some parts of our lives. That's different from lying to ourselves and to the Spirit. We lie when we claim to be completely led by the Spirit while still holding fast to an area of control.

📖 **Put an X on the line to indicate where you are in these parts of your life.**

Finances: _____

         Self-led   Spirit-led

Family relationships: _____

            Self-led   Spirit-led

Work: _____

   Self-led   Spirit-led

Leisure time: _____

        Self-led   Spirit-led

Sexual morality: _____

          Self-led   Spirit-led

Spiritual disciplines (prayer, worship, Bible study, praise, giving, witnessing, serving):

_____

Self-led   Spirit-led

I have often found myself preaching about a command of God that I failed to keep. I needed to be the first one to the altar to repent. When I was, the Spirit led me. When I was not, my pride and self got in the way. I am thankful that the Holy Spirit didn't strike me dead, but He had every right to do so.

EXPERIENCE THE HOLY SPIRIT

Surrendering the Lead

In dancing, the man usually leads, and the woman follows. In life, the Spirit always leads, and we always follow. Dancing in the Spirit can happen only when we surrender our natural (and sinful) inclination to lead, and then let the Holy Spirit lead.

Pray this prayer:

Spirit of God, take the lead in _____.
Help me to surrender my lead to You. I desire You to lead in every part of my life.
Amen.

Repeat this litany aloud and often for yourself:

At home,
where the Spirit leads, I will follow.
In church,
where the Spirit leads, I will follow.
At work,
where the Spirit leads, I will follow.
In finances,
where the Spirit leads, I will follow.
In family or marriage relationships,
where the Spirit leads, I will follow.
At play,
where the Spirit leads, I will follow.
In my thoughts, feelings, words, and actions,
where the Spirit leads, I will follow.

My Daily Walk in the Spirit

Review today's study. How willing are you to follow where the Spirit leads?

I will ask the Spirit to eliminate hypocrisy in the parts of my life that

_____

I know the Spirit is leading me when

_____

The part of my life that most desperately needs the Spirit's leading is

_____

Write a prayer thanking God's Spirit for how He has led you in the past.

_____

Write down this week's passage to memorize.

_____

Spiritual Truths

- Hypocrisy betrays parts of my life where the Spirit is not leading me.
- I must constantly surrender control to His leading.
- I avoid self-deception by following the lead of the Holy Spirit.

Day 5: The Spirit's River of Fire

Introduction

One of the symbols of the Holy Spirit in the New Testament is "rivers of living water" (John 7:38–39). Out of the throne of God flows His Spirit, the river of living water: "The angel showed me a pure river with the water of life, clear as crystal, flowing from the throne of God and of the Lamb" (Rev. 22:1).

Consider this: from the very throne flows the river of life, God's Spirit, into the depths of our beings as rivers of living water. Could it be that the very river of life (Gen. 2:10–14), which flowed in Eden and from which we were separated by the sin of the First Adam, has been restored to us through the Second Adam (Jesus) so that now everlasting life (Gal. 6:8) flows to and through us by the Spirit of God (John 7:38–39)?

This river of the Spirit flowing from the throne of God is also a river of fire—cleansing, purifying, and setting our hearts ablaze with a passionate love for Jesus.

Explore the Word

Ablaze Within

The Spirit's river of fire cleanses and purges all sin from our lives.

Read Daniel 7:9–10. In your own words describe the river of fire flowing from the throne of God.

Our lives are on fire. Jesus tells us that we are the light of the world (Matt. 5:14–16). In order for light to shine out of us, a fire must be burning within us. The fire comes from the Holy Spirit.

📖 **Read Acts 2.** Describe the fire of pentecost poured out on the early believers.

_____

📖 **Read Jeremiah 20:9.** Describe the fire burning within Jeremiah's bones.

_____

📖 **Read Deuteronomy 4:12.** Describe the voice of God that speaks from the fire.

_____

The fiery Holy Spirit burns within you, making of your life a consuming fire to set the world ablaze for Jesus.

EXAMINE YOURSELF

Are You Spiritually on Fire?

John Wesley is reputed to have prayed for God to set him on fire that others might see him burn. Are you on fire in that way? Will the fire of God's Spirit so consume you that everyone you meet will see the light of Jesus burning brightly in your life?

> W. E. Sangster of Westminster Central Hall was once a member of a group responsible for interviewing applicants for the Methodist ministry. A rather nervous young man presented himself before the group. The candidate said he felt he ought to explain that he was rather shy and was not the sort of person who would ever set the Thames River on fire, that is, create much of a stir in the city.

"My dear young brother," responded Sangster with insightful wit and wisdom, "I'm not interested to know if you can set the Thames on fire. What I want to know is this: If I picked you up by the scruff of your neck and dropped you into the Thames, would it sizzle?" (Quoted in *The Tale of the Tardy Oxcart* by Charles Swindoll [Nashville, TN: Word, 1998], 632)

Is there enough of the Spirit's river of fire flowing through you to produce sizzle in your life and the lives of others?

📖 **Describe how your life sizzles with the fire of the Spirit.**

EXPERIENCE THE HOLY SPIRIT

Invite His Fire

The river of fire may be just a trickle in your life. Unstop the well in your life and let His river flow. A chorus intones, "Burn in me, burn in me, let the fire of the Holy Ghost burn in me." Is that your prayer?

The consuming fire of God's Spirit will burn in your life upon your invitation.

📖 **Pray or sing:**

Holy Spirit, burn in me. Let Your river of fire flowing from the Father's throne now flow in me. Consume me with passion for Jesus and the zeal to tell everyone about His saving grace. Pour out Your tongues of fire upon me, even as You did that first pentecost. So light my life that all around me see Jesus—the Light of the World. Amen.

MY DAILY WALK IN THE SPIRIT

Review today's study. Flow in the Spirit's river of fire.

What has the Spirit's fire consumed in your life today?

_____

Describe how your zeal and passion inspired by the Spirit set another person on fire today.

_____

Write a prayer thanking God for His river of fire flowing through you.

_____

Write down what this week's passage to memorize means to you.

_____

SPIRITUAL TRUTHS

- The Spirit's river of fire flowing from the throne of God flows in me.

- I am set ablaze to burn brightly for Jesus.

- The source of all fiery zeal in my life comes from the Holy Spirit.

Week 7

THE SPIRIT'S PRESENCE COMFORTS, TEACHES, AND CONVICTS

I tried one self-paced, self-taught course through my years of schooling. How hard it was to stay focused and on track. Many distractions seemed to keep me from progressing satisfactorily through the course. I know that some people do very well with self-study courses. But even a self-study course requires a teacher to prepare the manual and teach the material through the written word or a computer program.

The Bible requires a Teacher. Living the Christian life requires a Guide. We are not in this alone. Jesus did not command us to follow Him and then abandon us to our own devices. We have a Guide into the future—the Holy Spirit.

When we face trials, tests, and tribulations, the Spirit is there to comfort and assure us. When we need to understand where we are or where we're going, the Holy Spirit instructs us with both wisdom and understanding. When we need to correct what's wrong in us or around us, the Spirit convicts us of sin and directs us in truth.

This week you will discover a Friend who sticks closer to you than any human being. You will walk with the eternal Companion who sustains you through every difficulty and exaltation in life.

You are not alone or helpless. The One who guides you also gives you strength for the journey, water for the dry places, and bread during times of spiritual famine. You will make it through, for He is with you.

This Week's Passage to Memorize

> I will ask the Father, and he will give you another Counselor, who will never leave you. He is the Holy Spirit, who leads into all truth. The world at large cannot receive him, because it isn't looking for him and doesn't recognize him. But you do, because he lives with you now and later will be in you. No, I will not abandon you as orphans—I will come to you. (JOHN 14:16–18)

Day 1: THE SPIRIT COUNSELS AND COMFORTS

INTRODUCTION

Earlier in the study, we learned that Jesus called the Holy Spirit "the Paraclete," which means both Counselor and Comforter. The Holy Spirit is the One who stands alongside us, guiding us through life, counseling us in all truth, and comforting us with the presence of God.

Jesus promised that He would be with us always (Matt. 28:20). He abides with us through the Spirit. The Holy Spirit is constantly telling us what He says (John 16:13–15) and guiding us in all truth.

In graduate school, I went through clinical training to be a pastoral counselor. I learned some of the qualities of a good counselor. Through the years, I have experienced that the Holy Spirit excels in all these qualities. A good counselor does the following:

- Listens without interrupting

- Understands the counselee's pain and suffering

- Empathizes without sympathizing

- Helps the counselee test his perceptions against the truth

- Comforts and encourages

- Builds up instead of tearing down

- Helps the counselee make his own decisions based on truth

Have you seen a commercial for a popular credit card? Adapting its approach, I might say to you:

- A personality test or inventory—$25

- A group session with a therapy group—$50

- A session with a counselor—$75

- A counseling session with the Holy Spirit—*Priceless!*

There are certainly times when it is beneficial to go to a counselor, but know that you always have by your side the Counselor of all ages—the Holy Spirit.

EXPLORE THE WORD

Has the Spirit Counseled You Lately?

When walking in the Spirit, we need daily counseling sessions with the Holy Spirit. He needs to be a part of every decision, conversation, action, thought, and feeling. Here are some of the questions we can constantly ask Him:

- Holy Spirit, how should I respond to that negative remark or behavior?

- Holy Spirit, what kind of food should I eat at this meal that will help my temple stay healthy?

- Holy Spirit, whom shall I tell today about Jesus?

- Holy Spirit, how shall I pray?

Like three-year-olds who love to learn about everything around them, we should ask endless questions. No question is too trivial or trite to ask the Holy Spirit.

Read the following scripture aloud. It records Jesus' words.

Yes, ask anything in my name, and I will do it! If you love me, obey my commandments. And I will ask the Father, and he will give you another Counselor, who will never leave you. He is the Holy Spirit, who leads into all truth. The world at large cannot receive him, because it isn't looking for him and doesn't recognize him. But you do, because he lives with you now and later will be in you. No, I will not abandon you as orphans—I will come to you. . . . But when the Father sends the Counselor as my representative—and by the Counselor I mean the Holy Spirit—he will teach you everything and will remind you of everything I myself have told you. I am leaving you with a gift—peace of mind and heart. And the peace I give isn't like the peace the world gives. So don't be troubled or afraid. (JOHN 14:14–18, 26–27)

Underline the phrases that you need the most or mean the most to you. Circle the words that answer the needs of your heart.

EXAMINE YOURSELF

Are You Taking His Counsel?

It's one thing to be counseled by the Holy Spirit. It's another to receive, obey, and follow His counsel. His counsel and wisdom may go against your human nature or the advice of others. Such counsel may cause you to feel uncomfortable. If you feel uncomfortable with the Spirit's counsel, how do you usually respond? (Circle the words that fit your response.)

- Frustrated
- Obedient
- Angry
- Worried

- Upset
- Challenged
- Other: _____

When the Spirit counsels us and we disobey, He often waits until we repent and obey before speaking to us about the next situation in our lives. If you are having a difficult time hearing the Spirit's counsel in a present circumstance, examine yourself and see if there is any recent counsel from the Spirit you have disobeyed that could be hindering His work in your life now.

EXPERIENCE THE HOLY SPIRIT

When Do You Need His Counsel?

Where do you run when you are afraid? To whom do you talk when you are upset? Who listens when you are working through a problem? Who cares for and comforts you when you are hurting? No human being can be there for you all the time. But the Holy Spirit can and will be there. Jesus promises that He will never leave you.

Complete these sentence prayers that apply to your life now:

Holy Spirit, help me conquer my fear of _____

Holy Spirit, hear my troubled cry about _____

Holy Spirit, help me solve _____

Holy Spirit, comfort me because I am hurting about_____

Holy Spirit, guide me in how to handle my relationship with _____

The Holy Spirit is as close as your next breath. He is waiting and ready to counsel and comfort you in every situation. Don't let anything keep you from asking for His priceless counsel.

My Daily Walk in the Spirit

Review what you have learned about and experienced in the Holy Spirit today.

The most important thing I learned about the Holy Spirit is

_____

The one thing on which I most critically need His counsel is

_____

The one area for which I need His help in praying is

_____

I ask the Holy Spirit to comfort me in

_____

Write a prayer thanking Jesus for giving you the Spirit who counsels and comforts you.

_____

Write the passage to memorize for this week.

_____

Spiritual Truths

- The Holy Spirit never leaves me and is always there to counsel me in truth.

- The Holy Spirit comforts me when no one else may care.

- I can tell the Holy Spirit anything, and He understands.

Day 2: THE SPIRIT CONVICTS

INTRODUCTION

Conviction is being told what's right even when it hurts. Conviction is finding out that I'm wrong even when I think I'm right. Conviction is learning the truth about myself. And there are times when no one has the courage to tell me the truth about myself except the Spirit of truth!

Years ago I believed the church to be my source and my abilities to be the strength I needed to do ministry. Yes, pride does come before a fall (Prov. 16:18). I mistakenly believed that I served the ministry instead of serving Christ. I thought that God needed my abilities to do ministry when He really needed my availability. The Holy Spirit continued to convict me of my sinful ways, but I wasn't listening. But one day He got my attention through a series of life-changing events and crises. The Holy Spirit convicted me of sin and taught me that God is my Source, I serve Christ and His people, not my ministerial career, and I need the gifts and fruit of the Spirit far more than any ability or talent I have.

When the Spirit convicts you, do you respond, repent, and begin anew, or do you carry the baggage of past sin and guilt around with you for a long time?

EXPLORE THE WORD

How Does the Spirit Convict?

The Holy Spirit uses the sword of God's Word to pierce our hearts when we sin. The writer of Hebrews declared, "For the word of God is full of living power. It is sharper than the sharpest knife, cutting deep into our innermost thoughts and desires. It exposes us for what we really are" (Heb. 4:12). And Paul told us that the sword of the Spirit is God's Word (Eph. 6:17).

So the Spirit uses the Word of God like a scalpel to cut out the cancerous sin in our lives.

Read John 16:6–15. Describe in your own words how the Holy Spirit convicts you of sin.

_____

 Read Hebrews 4:7. When the Spirit speaks to you with a convicting word, how do you respond?

_____

EXAMINE YOURSELF

How Does the Spirit Get Your Attention?

The Holy Spirit has many ways to get your attention and convict you of sin. How does He get through to you when you have sinned?

He gets your attention. Check all the different ways you have heard the voice of the Spirit convicting you of sin:

- ☐ In a sermon
- ☐ In a Bible study or lesson
- ☐ Through a Christian book or devotional
- ☐ Through a comment or conversation with a friend
- ☐ In the criticism of an enemy
- ☐ Through facing a crisis or problem
- ☐ Other: _____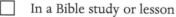

How do you respond when the Holy Spirit convicts you? At the top of the next page, put an X on the line near the phrase that represents your response.

Repent quickly	Deny sin
Confess honestly	Make excuses

The writer of Hebrews urged, "Today you must listen to his voice. Don't harden your hearts against him" (Heb. 4:7). When the Holy Spirit convicts, admit your sin, quit doing what's wrong, and then move on with your life, forgetting the past condemnation.

EXPERIENCE THE HOLY SPIRIT

Are You Listening to and Obeying the Spirit's Voice?

The Holy Spirit is talking to you. He doesn't want your answering machine or your voice mail. He wants a face-to-face, personal dialogue with you. His conviction brings you to repentance so that you will not be hindered by sin. He desires for you to grow and mature in Christ without returning to past bondages.

When the Spirit convicts, don't try to make things right with God by trying harder to keep the law and justify yourself.

Read Galatians 5:1, 4–5.

Doing what's right now doesn't cover up what's been wrong. The Spirit desires repentance, not self-righteousness.

One wall that keeps us from experiencing the Spirit is self-righteousness. When He convicts, we run to Him in repentance or away from Him in self-righteousness. Deep repentance brings a flow of the Holy Spirit into our lives.

Read Acts 3:19. If the Holy Spirit has been convicting you of sin and you've been avoiding repentance, write a prayer of repentance right now.

_____

Be assured that your repentance will not bring condemnation; confession brings forgiveness.

📖 **Read the following passages, and then complete the sentences.**

"God can use sorrow in our lives to help us turn away from sin and seek salvation. We will never regret that kind of sorrow. But sorrow without repentance is the kind that results in death" (2 Cor. 7:10).

The Holy Spirit has been using conviction and sorrow to turn me away from

_____

"If my people who are called by my name will humble themselves and pray and seek my face and turn from their wicked ways, I will hear from heaven and will forgive their sins and heal their land" (2 Chron. 7:14).

The Holy Spirit convicts me of pride and humbles me when

_____

"If we say we have no sin, we are only fooling ourselves and refusing to accept the truth. But if we confess our sins to him, he is faithful and just to forgive us and to cleanse us from every wrong. If we claim we have not sinned, we are calling God a liar and showing that his word has no place in our hearts" (1 John 1:8–10).

I confess that what keeps me from confessing my sin is

_____

With sincere repentance and continual confession comes the refreshing and renewing presence of the Holy Spirit.

My Daily Walk in the Spirit

📖 **Review what you have experienced and learned today in the Spirit.**

Describe how the Holy Spirit gets your attention and convicts you of sin.

_____

The next time you experience His conviction, how will you respond?

_____

When you repent, how does the Holy Spirit respond to you?

_____

Write a prayer asking God to do whatever is necessary to get your attention when you sin and bring you to repentance and renewal.

_____

Write down this week's passage to memorize, and describe what truth it has revealed to you during the week.

_____

Spiritual Truths

- The Holy Spirit lovingly, firmly, and immediately convicts me when I sin.

- My response to His conviction needs to be immediate repentance and confession.

- Self-righteousness and a failure to repent keep me from experiencing the refreshing of the Holy Spirit in my life.

Day 3: LISTENING TO JESUS THROUGH THE SPIRIT

INTRODUCTION

Overseas on the mission field, a friend of mine wanted to stay in touch with me and all of his intercessors in the States. However, that was in the days before E-mail. Since it was too expensive and time-consuming to write letters to everyone in the States who needed to hear from him, he sent one letter to a close associate in the States, and that person then wrote or faxed everyone, telling what was happening with our missionary colleague overseas.

Our associate here in the States who relayed all the information was a reliable and faithful communicator. Whatever he said was happening overseas to our missionary was always true and accurate. In many ways, his role was very similar to that of the Holy Spirit operating in our relationship with Jesus. The Holy Spirit listens to all that Jesus has to say as the word of God and then relays that word to us.

EXPLORE THE WORD

Getting the Message

When someone sends you an important letter, you may have to sign for it to certify its receipt. The Holy Spirit is the Lord's guarantee that you both receive and hear what He desires to say to you.

> **In each passage noted on the next page, Jesus explains how the Holy Spirit relays the truth about Himself to you.** Read each text and then describe what the Spirit is speaking to you.

"When the Father sends the Counselor as my representative—and by the Counselor I mean the Holy Spirit—he will teach you everything and will remind you of everything I myself have told you" (John 14:26).

What is the Holy Spirit teaching you now in your life? _____

_____

What is He reminding you about what Jesus said? _____

_____

"I will send you the Counselor—the Spirit of truth. He will come to you from the Father and will tell you all about me" (John 15:26).

What is the Holy Spirit telling you about Jesus? _____

_____

"All that the Father has is mine; this is what I mean when I say that the Spirit will reveal to you whatever he receives from me" (John 16:15).

What has the Holy Spirit been revealing to you? _____

_____

When you read Scripture, the One who inspired it—the Holy Spirit—will interpret it for you, applying biblical truth to your life. When you listen to sermons or teaching, pray, and spend time in worship, the Holy Spirit will speak to your life and reveal what the Lord is saying in the present moment.

EXAMINE YOURSELF

What Have You Heard from the Spirit?

You may need to keep a spiritual journal in order to record all that the Holy Spirit is saying to you about Jesus. That way, you will have a specific record of how the Spirit is leading your life. Try some of the ideas noted at the top of the next page.

Read the gospel of John. Look for all the "I am" passages. For example, Jesus says, "I am the living bread" (John 6:51). Let the Holy Spirit reveal to you how Jesus is the "I am" for every situation in your life.

Read the gospel of Mark. Look for all the miracles of Jesus. Let the Holy Spirit reveal to you how Jesus is doing miracles around and through you as your eyes are opened to see Him at work.

The Holy Spirit is your Teacher. He is the One continually helping you learn about Jesus. The Lord commanded, "Take my yoke upon you, and learn of me; for I am meek and lowly in heart: and ye shall find rest unto your souls. For my yoke is easy, and my burden is light" (Matt. 11:29–30 KJV). The only way to learn of Jesus is to study His Word, letting the Holy Spirit teach you and to be in a community of believers who are learning of Jesus and listening to the teaching of the Holy Spirit.

Describe how you are learning of Jesus this week through the Spirit.

_____

_____

_____

EXPERIENCE THE HOLY SPIRIT

Invite Him to Speak to You

The Holy Spirit constantly desires to teach and reveal to you the infinite truths about Jesus. He wants to speak to you whatever Jesus has for you right now. But you must be in a receiving and listening mode. Too often we are rushing through life without waiting on the Holy Spirit to tell us what He knows of Jesus.

Complete these sentences and tell the Holy Spirit when you will listen to Him:

Holy Spirit, I will read my Bible

_____

Holy Spirit, I will worship

_____

Holy Spirit, I will pray

_____

Holy Spirit, I will listen to teaching and preaching

_____

The Holy Spirit is speaking to you this moment about Jesus. Are you listening?

MY DAILY WALK IN THE SPIRIT

Review today's study. Whatever Jesus said that you need to remember, the Spirit will remind you today.

Write down what you are hearing about Jesus from the Spirit today.

_____

Write a prayer requesting the Holy Spirit to remind you daily that you need to listen to Him.

_____

Sit still for at least fifteen minutes. Focus your thoughts on the scriptures you read today. Listen to what the Holy Spirit tells you they mean. Write down what He tells you.

_____

Write down this week's passage to memorize.

_____

SPIRITUAL TRUTHS

- The Holy Spirit is constantly teaching me about Jesus.

- When I read the Word, I need to ask the Holy Spirit to reveal to me what it means and how to apply the Word to my life.

- I must take time to be still, then listen to and write down what the Spirit is telling me about Jesus.

Day 4: THE SPIRIT REVEALS THE FUTURE

INTRODUCTION

The only One who has been to our future is God. The devil doesn't know our future. Psychics cannot predict the future. Only God has been there, and only He knows what the future holds. The Holy Spirit will tell you the future (John 16:13). Are you consulting with Him first about your future?

Many people seem to fear the future. They worry about it, save for it, plan for it, and try to ensure against future calamity. One gospel song intones, "I don't know what the future holds, but I know who holds the future." How true. God holds your future safely and securely in His hands. So why are you worried?

📖 **Read Matthew 6:27–34.**

EXPLORE THE WORD

The Spirit Will Tell You About the Future
The Spirit-breathed Word of God has already revealed to you much about the future and how you are to respond.

📖 **Read the following scriptures, and write down how you are to respond to the future: John 16:13; Jeremiah 29:11–13; Matthew 6:25–34; 1 Corinthians 15; 1 Thessalonians 4:13–5:11; and 1 Peter 5:7.**

EXAMINE YOURSELF

How Do You Feel About Your Future?

So how do you feel about your future? Examine your feelings, and circle whatever feelings apply to your future.

- Worried

- Anxious

- Uncertain

- Hopeful

- Excited

- Good

- Pessimistic

- Encouraged

- Other: _____

Now go back over the list, and see how many negative feelings you circled. Surrender those feelings to the Holy Spirit. If you are reading a horoscope or seeking ungodly, even psychic, advice about your future, repent immediately, and surrender all your desires to know about the future to the Holy Spirit.

EXPERIENCE THE HOLY SPIRIT

Give Him Your Plans

Too often we try to plan our future and then expect God's Spirit to bless our plans. Jesus plainly teaches, "He [the Holy Spirit] will tell you about the future" (John 16:13).

> **Write down your future goals and plans.** Once you have written them down, surrender each of them to the Holy Spirit. Ask Him what your future is in Christ. You may have already counseled with the Holy Spirit about your future and what you write down has come from Him. But if any plans are not His, you need to surrender them so that only His plans for your future are guiding your steps.

The Holy Spirit knows and takes care of your future. Walk with Him into the future, leaving your cares and worries in the past.

My Daily Walk in the Spirit

Review today's study. Continually ask the Holy Spirit to advise you on your future.

Whatever you have not entrusted to the Holy Spirit about your future, write that down and turn it over to Him now.

_____

Write down what the Holy Spirit has revealed to you about your future.

_____

Write a prayer of thanksgiving about your future.

_____

Write down this week's passage to memorize.

_____

Spiritual Truths

- The Holy Spirit knows my future. His plans for me are good!

- I can give all my cares and worries about the future to Him.

- I must exchange my plans for the future for His plans.

Day 5: GUARD YOUR TONGUE

INTRODUCTION

To whom does your tongue belong? As you continue on your walk in the Spirit, you will come to understand that the power of life and death is in your tongue. Proverbs 18:21 affirms, "Those who love to talk will experience the consequences, for the tongue can kill or nourish life." You can speak life (which is of the Spirit) or death (which is of the flesh) into the lives of others.

Have you ever said something to a loved one that you regretted and then later apologized with the lame excuse, "I really didn't mean to say that"? If you didn't mean it, why did you say it? Out of the heart, the mouth speaks. What's in you is destined to come out of you.

EXPLORE THE WORD

You Can Speak the Spirit's Words

"The Holy Spirit will teach you what needs to be said even as you are standing there," Jesus promised (Luke 12:12). He was referring to the pressure of being judged and persecuted. Whenever you are under stress, you will speak either from the Spirit or from your flesh. What usually happens?

Complete these sentences:

When I'm unjustly accused, I usually_____

When I'm angry, I usually say_____

When I'm offended or hurt, I usually say _____

When I don't know what to say, I usually _____

When I'm fearful, I usually _____

What kinds of words come out of your mouth? The Holy Spirit will help you guard your tongue. You can speak the words of Jesus, which are eternal life to others.

> **Read John 6:63.** Describe where words of life come from.

_____

_____

> **Use a concordance.** Go through the book of Proverbs, and read all the passages about the tongue. Write down the advice from Proverbs that speaks to you about using your tongue.

_____

_____

EXAMINE YOURSELF

Who's in Control of Your Tongue?

At times such garbage may come from your tongue that you don't recognize your own voice. Does the Holy Spirit really have control of your tongue, or is your mouth speaking out of some stronghold in your flesh?

Think about the last week. List any people you may have offended with your tongue.

_____

_____

Now write a prayer repenting specifically of what you said to each person.

_____

_____

Describe how you will go to each person and ask forgiveness.

_____

_____

EXPERIENCE THE HOLY SPIRIT

Ask the Spirit to Speak Through You

Whenever you speak, the Holy Spirit is willing to fill your tongue with the Word of God and to help you guard your tongue from speaking death. However, you must surrender control of your tongue to the Spirit. Who needs to hear words of life from you today? Picture that person in your mind. Pray:

> *Holy Spirit, reveal to me the words of life You want me to speak to*
> _____.

Now ask the Holy Spirit to give you the words to speak. Write down what He tells you.

_____

_____

Within you is a river of life. Within you are words of life. Within you is everlasting life. The Holy Spirit deposited all there. Ask the Spirit to bring whatever is of Him out of you in all that you say!

My Daily Walk in the Spirit

Review today's study. Ask the Holy Spirit to put words of life on your tongue.

List the times this past week when you have spoken words of death to another person. Repent of those words.

_____

Write down the times you are most tempted to speak words of death instead of words of life.

_____

Write a prayer asking the Holy Spirit to remind you of words of life instead of death when you speak to others.

_____

Write down what this week's passage to memorize means to you.

_____

Spiritual Truths

- The Holy Spirit gives me words of life to speak to others.

- Through the Spirit's power, I can resist the temptation to speak words of death.

- The Holy Spirit can give me the right words to say in any situation if I ask Him.

Part 3

Be Empowered by the Spirit

Week 8

FLOWING IN THE SPIRIT

The river of God's Spirit flows from the throne of God into your spirit, overflowing into your mind, will, feelings, and actions. You are like a bubbling fountain, but unlike water in a recycling fountain, the source for you is the Spirit flowing into and out of your life.

Out of God's throne flows a river. John wrote about it in Revelation 22: "And the angel showed me a pure river with the water of life, clear as crystal, flowing from the throne of God and of the Lamb, coursing down the center of the main street. On each side of the river grew a tree of life, bearing twelve crops of fruit, with a fresh crop each month. The leaves were used for medicine to heal the nations" (vv. 1–2). The head of this river is God's throne. The destination of this river is you.

📖 **Read John 7:37–39.**

Have you ever felt drained in your spiritual life? Although you may feel something is wrong, your drained feeling may indicate something very positive and mature in your walk. As the river of God's Spirit flows out of you in ministry and serving others, you need to be filled and replenished spiritually. The Holy Spirit does not leave you empty and dry. The river of the Spirit flows from the Father and Son into you. The Spirit's river flows continuously without limit from God. You can block the flow, but He never leaves or abandons you. So tap into the flow of the Spirit.

This Week's Passage to Memorize

> "If you believe in me, come and drink! For the Scriptures declare that rivers of living water will flow out from within." (When he said "living water," he was speaking of the Spirit, who would be given to everyone believing in him. But the Spirit had not yet been given, because Jesus had not yet entered into his glory.) (JOHN 7:38–39)

Day 1: THE FOUNTAIN WITHIN

INTRODUCTION

The Holy Spirit flowing within you continually refreshes and renews your walk in the Spirit. A car needs more gasoline to continue down the road. A light needs more electricity to burn brightly. A body needs more water to continue to live. Your spirit needs more of the Spirit to continue to walk in the Spirit.

Your walk in the Spirit will grow stagnant and stale without the continual flow of the Spirit in your life. Certain dams in your life can restrict or limit the flow of the Holy Spirit within you. Today and throughout this week, you will identify things that can restrict the Spirit's flow as well as uncover things that can open you to His refreshing and renewing in your life.

Like every relationship, your walk with the Spirit has ups and downs. Unlike the individuals in other relationships, however, the Holy Spirit never lets you down. If you feel farther away from the Holy Spirit today than yesterday or last week, guess who's moved. You have!

EXPLORE THE WORD

Allow the River to Flow

Living water comes from Jesus Himself. And He sends that water into your life through the Holy Spirit. Without water, we physically die. Without the living water of the Holy Spirit, we spiritually die.

> **Read what Jesus says about living water in John 7:37–39, and then describe what His living water does in a believer's life.**

Throughout Scripture, God promises to refresh us with springs and rivers of living water. Read these passages, and write down how the Spirit of God refreshes us with living water.

Psalm 42:1–2: _____

Psalm 63:1–7: _____

Psalm 107:31–35: _____

Proverbs 21:1–2: _____

Isaiah 35:4–7: _____

Isaiah 41:17–18: _____

Isaiah 44:1–6: _____

Jeremiah 17:13–14: _____

Ezekiel 47: _____

Hebrews 10:21–23: _____

1 John 5:1–11: _____

EXAMINE YOURSELF

What Stops the Flow?

You can dam up the Spirit's river flowing through your life. On the one side, you can stop the flow by withdrawing from intimacy with the Holy Spirit.

Check any of the river's dams that you have experienced in your life recently:

☐ Prayerlessness

☐ Lack of time for reading, studying, and meditating on the Word

☐ Too little fellowship and accountability with other believers

☐ Shallow/superficial worship

☐ Other: _____

On the other side, you can dam up the river's flow by not letting Him flow out of your life into your relationships through serving and loving others.

Check any of the river's dams that keep the Spirit from flowing out of you now:

☐ Lack of loving and serving others in Jesus' name   ☐ Offense

☐ Impurity   ☐ Unforgiveness

☐ Self-centeredness   ☐ Bitterness

☐ Anger   ☐ Doubt

☐ Depression   ☐ Unconfessed sin

☐ Hopelessness   ☐ Other: _____

EXPERIENCE THE HOLY SPIRIT

Remove the Impediments to His Flow

You can unstop the river and release the Holy Spirit. One night as I lay awake in bed reflecting on recent sin in my life, a flood of guilt and remorse washed over me. For hours I allowed the condemnation of the accuser (Rev. 12) to beat me up. I wondered whether some of the sin habits in my thoughts and actions would ever be broken. I wept over the missed opportunities I had sidestepped as a result of sinful blind spots in my life.

Has this ever happened to you? Have you allowed yourself to become mired in the bog of sin and guilt with waves of inadequacy and condemnation crashing over your spirit?

Describe a time when you dwelled on your sin and failures as a Christian. Also tell how the Spirit helped you through and out of sin's miry bog.

_____

As I lay there drowning in self-pity and self-recriminations, the Holy Spirit suddenly jolted me with a revelation from Romans 8:1–2. He reminded me that I was not under condemnation. He asked me, *Why do you let your heart condemn you when I have forgiven you?*

📖 **Read 1 John 1:19 and 1 John 3:19–22. What is God's promise to you?**

_____

_____

Here's the bottom line. You can experience conviction and repent quickly, receiving God's forgiveness, or you can hold on to sin and experience unnecessary condemnation and guilt. If you have restricted or stopped the Spirit's river from flowing in your life for any reason, confess that to the Lord right now. Your repentance will be the dynamite that levels any dam stopping the river's flow.

📖 **Write a prayer confessing any dam of the Spirit in your life.**

_____

_____

My Daily Walk in the Spirit

Review today's study. Let the Spirit's river flow freely in your life.

Describe what you will do to keep the dams from forming in your life that impede the Spirit's flow.

_____

When you experience self-condemnation in the future, how will you respond to this spiritual attack?

_____

Write a prayer inviting the Spirit's river to flow without hindrance in your life.

_____

Write down this week's passage to memorize.

_____

Spiritual Truths

- I need to destroy all the hindrances to the Spirit's river in my life.

- The Holy Spirit desires to flow into me with continual refreshing and out of me with continual loving and serving.

- When I face self-condemnation, I can repent quickly and continue in the flow of the Holy Spirit.

Day 2: TRUE WORSHIP

INTRODUCTION

The Holy Spirit flows in worship. He flows into us and out of us. Without His presence in worship, all that we sing, say, and do is lifeless ritual. Have you ever felt as if you were simply going through the motions in worship? The songs were empty melodies. The prayers were vain repetitions. The words were empty phrases. And the place where you found yourself was cold, empty, and lonely, even in a crowd of people.

Often we blame the preacher, the choir, or the church as a whole for our emptiness in worship. But we must look first at our hearts. Are we worshiping in spirit and in truth? Is the living water of the Holy Spirit actually flowing into us, through us, and back to the Lord in praise and worship?

Worship is a key to your walk in the Spirit. Jesus emphasized, "You must worship the Lord your God; serve only him" (Matt. 4:10). Your intimacy with the Holy Spirit will be reflected in the depth and intensity of your worship.

EXPLORE THE WORD

Worship in Spirit and in Truth

A Samaritan woman met Jesus at a well. She came to draw water for physical thirst, but only God could meet her real thirst. Hurt and rejection dammed up any spiritual river in her life. Five men had divorced her, and the one she lived with wouldn't marry her. But the seventh man she met had living water to satisfy the deep yearnings of her soul.

Read John 4. Complete these sentences:

What the woman really needed from Jesus was _____

What Jesus promised was _____

Jesus described living water as _____

Jesus insisted that true, living worship is _____

Because we know the Source of living water, Jesus, we can ask Him for the living water of the Spirit to flow from His throne into our lives. Out of living water flows true worship. The Spirit reveals the Father's love to us. The Spirit lifts up the saving grace of Jesus Christ. The Spirit inspires our thanksgiving, praise, and worship of the triune God who loves and saves us.

EXAMINE YOURSELF

Is My Worship True?

Truth refers to an absolute consistency between your inner self and your outer behavior. Truth points to a transparency in your life so that the real you is exposed to His light. The Spirit uses truth to cut away all religion and expose your heart in worship. How true is your worship?

Examine your worship. On a scale of 0 (completely missing) to 5 (overflowing abundantly), examine your worship life:

Filled with joy, praise, and adoration	0 1 2 3 4 5
Thirsting and hungering after God	0 1 2 3 4 5
Transparent, honest, and real	0 1 2 3 4 5
Passionately in love with Jesus	0 1 2 3 4 5
Empowered by the Holy Spirit	0 1 2 3 4 5

If elements are missing from your worship, you need to return to the Source, the headwaters of worship—the Holy Spirit.

📖 **Read Romans 12:1–2.** Summarize Paul's description of true worship.

_____

Are you willing to make the living sacrifice that true worship requires?

EXPERIENCE THE HOLY SPIRIT

Let the Spirit Flow in Your Worship

True worship flows out of your intimacy with the Holy Spirit. He will teach you how to praise God and adore Jesus. He will develop your appetite for more of the Bread of Life. The Spirit will intensify your longing for the Lord.

Take time alone with the Holy Spirit each day. Find a praise and worship CD that helps you fix your eyes on Jesus in worship. Sing with the music. Let the Holy Spirit begin to worship through you by inviting His river to flow. Put away all distractions. Spend one-on-one time just with Him.

If your worship has become shallow and superficial, you may need to do the following (check all that apply):

☐ I need to involve myself with a more worshipful community of faith.

☐ I need to spend personal worship time daily with the Lord.

☐ I need to invite the Holy Spirit to flow through me as I worship.

☐ I need to ask the Holy Spirit to teach me how to worship.

☐ Other: _____

📖 **Write a prayer to follow through on the statements you have checked.**

_____

Without the Holy Spirit, true worship is impossible. In the Spirit, worship becomes a living sacrifice.

My Daily Walk in the Spirit

Review today's study. The Holy Spirit invites you to worship in spirit and in truth.

One way my worship has deepened and grown recently is

_____

One way my worship in the Spirit needs to grow is

_____

I pray that as I worship, I will

_____

Write down this week's passage to memorize.

_____

Spiritual Truths

- The Holy Spirit helps me worship the Father in spirit and in truth.

- I can invite the Holy Spirit to fill and overflow my worship of the Lord.

- The Holy Spirit will deepen my desire to worship God.

Day 3: SPRING UP, O WELL

INTRODUCTION

The Holy Spirit is a fountain of living water springing up within you and flowing out of your life in service and ministry. You can't give what you don't have. And you don't have anything to give in service, ministry, or worship without the Holy Spirit.

Have you ever had times in life when the well has run dry? You've started to pray, and *nothing*. You've begun to worship, and *nothing*. You've wanted to give, and *nothing*. You know that you've needed to study the Word, but the words stick to the page and *nothing* enters your mind or spirit. What's happened? Something has clogged the well. What's needed? It's time to dig a new well.

Your inner self feeds on the Word of God. The Spirit in you flows out of you as you walk in the Spirit. But there are times in life when you enter into a spiritual wasteland where all seems spiritually arid and dry. Today it's time to discover how to dig a new well.

EXPLORE THE WORD

Digging New Wells

Read Genesis 26, which tells the story of Isaac's need to dig new wells. Retell the story in your own words, and describe why Isaac needed to dig new wells.

📖 **Read Numbers 21, which tells the story of Israel's need for a new well.** What did Israel do to secure fresh water?

_____

As you have discovered, living water represents the presence of God's Spirit. Wells are one way the flow of that living water in your life can be understood as you walk in the Spirit.

📖 **Read the following passage, and write down what it says about needing fresh water from new wells.**

Isaiah 12:1–3:

_____

EXAMINE YOURSELF

Is Your Well Clogged?

Whatever may clog your well from time to time needs to be removed. And there are times when you need to dig a new well or stop drinking from someone else's well. For example, some people try to live vicariously off what the latest writer, preacher, televangelist, or teacher has springing up in his well. As deep as that well may be and as refreshing as the splash of that experience of the Spirit may be for you, your relationship with the Spirit cannot live off someone else's water.

To dig a well, you must shovel away the dirt that clogs the Spirit's pipeline to your body and soul.

📖 **Complete these sentences:**

What's clogging my well is

_____

_____

I need a new well to spring up in

_____

EXPERIENCE THE HOLY SPIRIT

Dig a New Well

You may need to dig a new well into a spiritual discipline, which has the Spirit's waters as its source, that will release a fresh spring of living water into your life. For example, you may dig a new well down deep into praise so that the praise that bubbles up in you will flow afresh from Him. Or you may dig deep into the soils of

- the Word for fresh revelation.

- fasting for newfound discipline over body and soul.

- giving to stir the waters of generosity.

- worship to bathe in His presence.

- dreams and visions to see His plan more clearly.

- faith that you may walk in the invisible.

- prayer so that God and you may commune more intimately.

- witnessing so that His Spirit will renew your testimony.

- service to embrace afresh the Suffering Servant's attitude.

- silence so that you may unmistakably hear His voice.

Review the list. Underline the soils into which you most need to dig a new well.

New wells dug into good soil tap into springs of living water that help us flow to a deeper level of intimacy with the Holy Spirit. Pray,

Spring up, O well of the Spirit, in the dry places of my life. Amen.

My Daily Walk in the Spirit

📖 **Review today's study.** Get ready to dig some new wells in your life.

What wells have you unclogged this week?

_____

What new wells have you dug?

_____

Write a prayer asking the Holy Spirit to uncover new springs of living water in your life.

_____

Write down this week's passage to memorize.

_____

Spiritual Truths

- Sin clogs the Spirit's wells in my life.

- I must constantly unclog my wells.

- Digging into good soil, I can tap the fresh, living water of new wells in the Spirit.

Day 4: STREAMS IN THE DESERT

INTRODUCTION

The Spirit led Jesus into the desert to be tempted. God led Israel into the wilderness to be taught and tested before entering the promised land. Not all trials arise from our sin or the enemy's attacks. As you walk in the Spirit, some of your desert and wilderness experiences will arise from the leading of the Holy Spirit: "Then Jesus was led out into the wilderness by the Holy Spirit to be tempted there by the Devil. For forty days and forty nights he ate nothing and became very hungry" (Matt. 4:1–2).

So why does the Spirit lead us into deserts? Why does He allow wilderness experiences? One reason is to refine our faith (1 Peter 1). Another is perhaps more subtle. The desert causes us to thirst more for the Spirit's living water. At times my satiation dulls my sense of dependence on and need of the Holy Spirit. Living beside a pure, sparkling mountain stream, I might take for granted its presence and refreshing in my life. But put me on a trek in the desert under a hot, scorching sun, and my thirst increases exponentially. Thoughts of that cool, refreshing mountain stream surge through my brain. I see that water in mirages and desperately desire to drink from it.

So it is with the Spirit. The more I find myself in the wilderness or desert, the more aware I become of my need for and dependence on Him.

EXPLORE THE WORD

There Will Be Springs in Your Desert

God promises that water will spring forth in the desert. Whenever you go through a desert experience, you can trust God's Spirit to be with you and to refresh you on the journey.

📖 **Read the following text, and underline every phrase of promise from God.**

Say to those who are afraid, "Be strong, and do not fear, for your God is coming to destroy your enemies. He is coming to save you." And when he comes, he will open the eyes of the blind and unstop the ears of the deaf. The lame will leap like a deer, and those who cannot speak will shout and sing! Springs will gush forth in the wilderness, and streams will water the desert. The parched ground will become a pool, and springs of water will satisfy the thirsty land. Marsh grass and reeds and rushes will flourish where desert jackals once lived. And a main road will go through that once deserted land. It will be named the Highway of Holiness. Evil-hearted people will never travel on it. It will be only for those who walk in God's ways; fools will never walk there. (ISA. 35:4–8)

The Holy Spirit walks with you on the Highway of Holiness. Even when that highway goes through a deserted land, He will be with you and will provide springs in your desert.

EXAMINE YOURSELF

When You're in the Desert . . .
As you thirst for the Holy Spirit, what do you do to satisfy that thirst?

📖 **Describe how you satisfy your thirst for the Spirit in your walk.**

_____

If you rage against the desert, wanting as Israel did to return to Egypt, you will find yourself worshiping idols and rebelling against God's Spirit. But if you look for His Highway of Holiness through the desert, you will come upon oases, manna, and meat for the journey. Rage and rebellion will blind you to His provision. Thirsting and hungering after Him will bring you to springs in the desert.

To what oasis has the Spirit led you in the past when you have walked through the desert?

_____

EXPERIENCE THE HOLY SPIRIT

Drink of His Water

Are your eyes open to the Holy Spirit's provisions in your desert? Part of the blessing of being led into the wilderness is discovering just how awesome and wonderful the living water of the Spirit is.

Write a prayer of thanksgiving to the Spirit for all the oases He has provided in the past.

_____

If you are presently walking through a desert, write a prayer telling the Holy Spirit how much you thirst for and depend on Him.

_____

Notice that the Highway of Holiness goes through the desert. The purpose of being led into and through the desert is not to break you but to drive you to an unquenchable thirst for the Spirit.

MY DAILY WALK IN THE SPIRIT

Review today's study. Only the Spirit can quench your thirst.

What streams in the desert have you discovered this week?

_____

Describe how you thirst for the Holy Spirit right now.

_____

Note some recent highlights of your journey along the Highway of Holiness.

_____

Write a prayer asking that the Spirit intensify your thirst and desire for His living streams.

_____

Write down this week's passage to memorize.

_____

SPIRITUAL TRUTHS

- As the Spirit leads me through the wilderness, He will provide streams of living water from which to drink.

- If I rage against the desert, I may miss what the Spirit is doing in my life.

- The Holy Spirit will satisfy every thirst I have for Him along the Highway of Holiness.

Day 5: At His Throne

INTRODUCTION

Have you imagined that you must wait until you get to heaven to drink of the river of life? Could it be that you must thirst without any taste until that day when you see Him face-to-face? Good news. You can begin to drink of the Spirit's river now.

Yes, now you will drink in part and then fully. Now you will be satisfied, only to thirst again; then you will never thirst again. Now you will journey from oasis to oasis; then you will dwell on the banks of the river. Now you will swim occasionally in the river; then you will be continually immersed by His flow.

EXPLORE THE WORD

Come to the River

I want you to see a progression of scriptures so that you will understand your access to the Spirit's river.

Read each scripture, and jot down how it relates to each step.

Step 1: You may boldly access His throne. Hebrews 10:19–22:

_____

Step 2: Out of His throne flows the river of life. Revelation 22:1–2:

_____

Step 3: You are in the heavenlies at the river. Ephesians 2:1–7:

_____

Step 4: Get into the river until you swim. Ezekiel 47:1–5; Acts 1:5:

_____

Swimming in the river of the Spirit is more than an eschatological hope; it's a present reality!

EXAMINE YOURSELF

Are You Swimming?

We may fear too much of a good thing, but when that good thing is the river of God's Spirit, we will never experience enough in this lifetime. In high school, I taught swimming and lifesaving for the Red Cross. I vividly remember the terror in the eyes of some children who were afraid of the water. Yet others eagerly jumped the first time into my outstretched arms, completely trusting me to save them from drowning.

How willing are you to jump into the river of God?

_____

EXPERIENCE THE HOLY SPIRIT

Jump In!

You have nothing to fear. Of course, the water will be over your head, just as it was over Peter's head when he walked toward Jesus. But Jesus is always there to baptize you with just what you need from the Holy Spirit. He desires to immerse you in His presence so that you might drink in the fullness of His love and grace.

Write a prayer asking Jesus to immerse you in the river of the Spirit.

_____

You have begun a journey through life's desert on the Highway of Holiness. Whenever you desire, take the plunge into the living water.

My Daily Walk in the Spirit

Review today's study. Let the deep in you cry out for the depths of the Spirit.

How have you experienced the river of God's Spirit in your life?

_____

When does what's deep in you cry out most for the depths of God's Spirit?

_____

Pray in the Spirit. Let the depths of you cry out for the depths of Him.

_____

What does this week's passage to memorize mean to you?

_____

Spiritual Truths

- The river of God's Spirit flows from His throne and into me.

- I can go into the depths of God as far as my desire takes me.

- Jesus desires to immerse (baptize) me with the river of the Spirit.

Week 9

GIFTED BY THE SPIRIT FOR MIRACLES, SIGNS, AND WONDERS

Empowered by the Holy Spirit, the early Christians walked in the miraculous. They boldly witnessed to the risen presence of Jesus in their midst. Of course, the Spirit did through them exactly what Jesus had promised,

> Just believe that I am in the Father and the Father is in me. Or at least believe because of what you have seen me do. The truth is, anyone who believes in me will do the same works I have done, and even greater works, because I am going to be with the Father. You can ask for anything in my name, and I will do it, because the work of the Son brings glory to the Father. Yes, ask anything in my name, and I will do it! (JOHN 14:11–14)

Consider time for a moment. You and I physically live in time and space, in what we call the temporal (i.e., the natural). But within us dwells the Spirit of God. Not only does the Spirit move in time and space, but He is eternal (i.e., supernatural). The Greek word for the usual passage of time is *chronos,* from which we get the word *chronometer.* But when the eternal invades the temporal, that moment in time is *chairos,* from which we get the word *crisis.* An interesting point is that the two symbols in Chinese representing crisis are *risk* and *opportunity.*

When the Holy Spirit invades time and space, *chairos* moments of miracles, signs, and wonders happen. They happen within you because the Spirit indwells you. They happen all around you because the Spirit in you is overflowing into the lives and events surrounding you. You are a miracle waiting to happen. When you enter into a situation or relationship, you bring the presence of the Holy Spirit with you. Signs and wonders will follow you.

This week, you will discover how the Holy Spirit baptizes you with power to do the works of Jesus in time and space. Miracles happen around you every day if you have the

Spirit's eyes to see and ears to hear. Jesus baptizes you (Acts 1–2) with the power of the Holy Spirit so that you might minister in His name wherever you go. As His power flows through you bringing *chairos* into your life, you will discover that it's risky living for Jesus. But a life filled with *chairos* moments is also overflowing with opportunities to bring the Spirit's power to save, heal, and deliver to all those you meet.

This Week's Passage to Memorize

Go into all the world and preach the Good News to everyone, everywhere. Anyone who believes and is baptized will be saved. But anyone who refuses to believe will be condemned. These signs will accompany those who believe: They will cast out demons in my name, and they will speak new languages. They will be able to handle snakes with safety, and if they drink anything poisonous, it won't hurt them. They will be able to place their hands on the sick and heal them. (MARK 16:15–18)

Day 1: Signs and Wonders Are for Now!

Introduction

As I walked into her hospital room, I expected to pray with the elderly woman before her surgery to remove kidney stones. She greeted me with a smile and immediately asked me to pray with her to be healed. "God's going to heal me," she exclaimed, brimming over with faith and confidence.

I was unsure about how to ask the Spirit to pray through me. So I began praying for her healing if it was God's will. She interrupted my prayer and informed me that God was going to heal her. Then her anesthesiologist entered the room and informed her that soon they would come to take her to surgery. She insisted on another set of X rays. She believed that God had healed her, and the X rays would confirm that she didn't need the surgery. Informing him that her pastor had agreed with her in prayer and now she was healed, she bewildered the anesthesiologist with her faith and stubbornness. No way would she go to surgery. She was healed!

The doctor finally relented to her demands and had X rays taken. They proved that her kidneys were free of the stones that had caused her enormous pain just a few days before. She was exuberant and gave glory to God for her healing (and her pastor's prayers) to everyone who came into her room—aides, nurses, friends, and doctors. It was really the first time I had prayed in agreement (Matt. 18:19) with anyone believing for her healing. I must admit that my faith had been the size of a mustard seed or smaller. But the truth remained that God was the Healer, not me or my prayers, and that a wonderful miracle had been performed for His glory.

EXPLORE THE WORD

The Spirit Acts with Signs and Wonders

Earlier in this study we examined the book of Acts and saw how the Holy Spirit did signs and wonders in the early church. Let's review for a moment.

📖 **Survey Acts 1–8. List every miracle, sign, and wonder recorded there.**

_____

The question for you is this: Do you believe that the Holy Spirit performs miracles, signs, and wonders today, just as He did in the early church? If not, why not? If so, are you witnessing His signs and wonders all around you? The Holy Spirit is at work all around you invading *chronos* with *chairos*. Are you seeing Him at work?

Not only is the Spirit at work all around you; He is at work in you to accomplish His goodwill. His power is at work in and through you to accomplish mighty things.

📖 **Read John 14:1–18.** List all of Jesus' promises in this passage.

_____

Jesus promised that we would do mighty works as He did and even greater works. Jesus also promised to give us the Holy Spirit as our Source, Counsel, Guide, and Strength for doing what He commands.

EXAMINE YOURSELF

What's Happening?

How is *chairos* being manifested in your life? What are you seeing the Holy Spirit do through you to save, heal, and deliver people?

📖 **Complete the sentences at the top of the next page.**

The most recent miracle of salvation I have witnessed is _____

The most recent miracle of healing I have witnessed is _____

The most recent miracle of deliverance I have witnessed is _____

The Holy Spirit delivers people bound by addictions, sinful habits, curses, demonic control, and religious bondages. Have you seen Him at work through your life to release God's power into time and space (*chronos*)?

If you haven't seen the Holy Spirit doing signs and wonders, could you be the problem because of one of these problems?

- Doubt
- Lukewarmness
- Love grown cold

- Prayerlessness
- Busyness
- Other: _____

 Circle any of the problems listed that apply to your life right now.

EXPERIENCE THE HOLY SPIRIT

Greater Works

Imagine this: the same resurrection power in the Holy Spirit that worked through Jesus also works in you—and in greater measure. What signs and wonders does the Holy Spirit want to do in your life today?

_____

 Write a prayer asking the Holy Spirit to reveal to you the signs and wonders He desires to do through you today.

_____

_____

When you do not ask Him to work through you performing signs and wonders, then someone who needs saving, healing, or delivering may miss God's miracle for his life because of your disobedience.

MY DAILY WALK IN THE SPIRIT

Review today's study. Who is waiting for a miracle on the other side of your obedience to the Spirit?

For whom is the Holy Spirit telling you to pray to receive a miracle today?

_____

What "greater work" has the Holy Spirit told you to do that still needs to be done?

_____

Write a prayer thanking Jesus for giving the Spirit to empower you to do the ministry He requires of you.

_____

Write down this week's passage to memorize.

_____

SPIRITUAL TRUTHS

- Jesus has given me the Spirit to perform signs and wonders.

- If I fail to see signs and wonders following me, I must be stifling the Spirit in my life.

- I must constantly be aware that there are people waiting for their miracles on the other side of my obedience to the Spirit's leading.

Day 2: KNOWING WHAT TO DO IN THE SPIRIT

INTRODUCTION

It's one thing to know that the power of God's Spirit dwells in you to do signs and wonders. It's quite another thing to know what "greater works" the Spirit wants you to do in Jesus' name. Operating in signs and wonders without the Spirit's wisdom and revelation is very dangerous to you spiritually and even physically, as you will discover in today's study.

Jesus promised that you would do greater works than He, and He also promised that the Holy Spirit would lead you in all truth. To understand what Jesus meant, you must first understand how He operated in the power of the Spirit. Jesus never did anything that the Father had not first revealed to Him. Jesus said, "I assure you, the Son can do nothing by himself. He does only what he sees the Father doing. Whatever the Father does, the Son also does. For the Father loves the Son and tells him everything he is doing, and the Son will do far greater things than healing this man. You will be astonished at what he does" (John 5:19–20).

Jesus told others only what the Father told Him to say (John 14:10). Whatever you do or say in His name must be done or said because the Spirit revealed it to you. Likewise, if you are to do greater works than Jesus did (John 14:12), then the Spirit of wisdom and revelation must reveal them to you.

EXPLORE THE WORD

Be Led by the Spirit of Wisdom and Revelation

In the book of Acts, we read of how the sons of Sceva decided to perform signs and wonders without the Spirit's power or leading. The results for them were disastrous.

Read Acts 19:11–20. Summarize what happened to the sons of Sceva.

_____

Notice in this narrative that the power of the Holy Spirit was not magic. Magic tried to manipulate the supernatural so that natural events were altered and man received power and glory. Miracles are always done by the Spirit according to the Father's will so that Jesus receives glory and honor. Praying, saying Jesus' name, or doing any kind of religious ritual can never manipulate the Holy Spirit into manifesting His power through signs and wonders.

Read Acts 8:17–25. Describe what Simon learned about the miracle-working power of the Spirit.

_____

You are not seeking signs and wonders. They accompany or follow you as you walk in the Spirit.

EXAMINE YOURSELF

Let the Spirit of Wisdom and Revelation Lead You
The only way to do what the Father does and to say what the Father wants you to say is to be led by the Spirit. He must reveal to you what the Father is doing and saying. The only way this will happen is for you to spend time in prayer receiving instructions from the Spirit through the Word.

Ask yourself these questions:

How am I praying for the Spirit to perform signs and wonders through me? _____

_____

What is my motivation for wanting signs and wonders to follow me? _____

_____

Two motivations dwell in the hearts of believers who desire signs and wonders to follow them. The first is to glorify the name of Jesus. The second is to exhibit the compassion of Jesus for those who need to be saved, healed, and delivered.

EXPERIENCE THE HOLY SPIRIT

Pray for the Spirit

The mighty power of God will work in and through you, performing signs and wonders through the Spirit of wisdom and revelation. Apart from the Holy Spirit, you can do nothing: "It is not by force nor by strength, but by my Spirit, says the LORD Almighty" (Zech. 4:6).

Paul's prayer in Ephesians 1:16–23 can now be applied to your life.

This prayer has been adapted for another believer to pray over you, putting your name in the blanks. This person could be a spouse, parent, child, pastor, elder, or another Christian who agrees in prayer with you for the Holy Spirit to work powerfully in your life.

I have not stopped giving thanks for _____, remembering _____ in my prayers. I keep asking that the God of our Lord Jesus Christ, the glorious Father, may give _____ the Spirit of wisdom and revelation, so that _____ may know Him better. I pray also that the eyes of _____'s heart may be enlightened in order that _____ may know the hope to which He has called _____, the riches of His glorious inheritance in the saints, and His incomparably great power for us who believe. That power is like the working of His mighty strength, which He exerted in Christ when He raised Him from the dead and seated Him at His right hand in the heavenly realms, far above all rule and authority, power and dominion, and every title that can be given, not only in the present age but also in the one to come. And God placed all things under His feet and appointed Him to be head over everything for the church, which is His body, the fullness of Him who fills everything in every way. Amen. (See EPH. 1:16–23 NIV.)

As you are filled with His wonder-working power, you will witness signs and wonders following your walk in the Spirit.

My Daily Walk in the Spirit

Review today's study. Sign and wonders follow you when you are led by the Spirit of wisdom and revelation.

What is the Spirit of wisdom and revelation leading you to say and do today?

_____

How is Jesus receiving glory in your life today?

_____

Write a prayer thanking Jesus for the power of the wonder-working Spirit in your life.

_____

Write down this week's passage to memorize.

_____

Spiritual Truths

- The Holy Spirit fills me with His power to do signs and wonders.

- My motivation must always be for His glory.

- The signs and wonders that follow me point others to Jesus, not to me.

Day 3: PROPHETIC SIGNS—GIVEN TO EDIFY

INTRODUCTION

When the Holy Spirit gifts you with power to minister to and serve others, He intends for you to build people up instead of tear people down. One powerful gift of the Spirit is that of prophecy. However, this gift is also subject to both abuse and control.

Over the years I have heard believers speak prophetically both corporately, to the church as a whole, and individually. Most prophetic words minister powerfully and miraculously in the lives of believers, helping to confirm what the Holy Spirit is doing or is preparing to do in their lives. However, there are times when prophetic words may be harmful. Instead of being a sign or wonder pointing someone to the Lord, they may be judgmental, misleading, or hurtful.

Well-meaning believers seeking to walk in the Spirit have spoken prophetic words to me or my family that have simply missed God's purpose and direction for our lives. At other times, the prophetic word worked miraculously in our lives to point us in God's way or correct a wrong direction.

EXPLORE THE WORD

Intended to Strengthen

One purpose of signs and wonders that are gifted by the Spirit is to glorify God. Another purpose is to edify, strengthen, comfort, and encourage others. If a person is using the power of spiritual gifts to control, manipulate, dominate, or intimidate others, that power is *not* of the Holy Spirit.

Examine the following scriptures. Write down what they say about spiritual gifts and their purpose, particularly the gift of prophecy.

1 Corinthians 14:3–5, 12, 24–26: _____

1 Corinthians 12:7: _____

1 Corinthians 13:1–2: _____

1 Thessalonians 5:19–21: _____

A wonderful sign or wonder in your life may be a prophetic word given to you that reveals God's purpose and intention in something happening in your life at that moment. Again, don't run after the sign or wonder for yourself, and don't seek such prophetic signs as gifts to "wow" others.

EXAMINE YOURSELF

What Does Prophecy Mean to You?

At times, you may be so desperately seeking the Spirit's guidance that you are running after a prophetic sign as pagans seek a psychic. Beware. The Holy Spirit is at work all around you, but so is the demonic. Satan wants to lie to you and steal from you. He may be at work through another person to mislead or deceive you.

When a prophetic word comes to me, I judge it by_____

When I am given a prophetic word, I test it by _____

When a prophetic word is fulfilled in my life, my response is_____

 How do you test prophetic words you have for others or others have for you?

Asking the following questions may test the words. Check the ones that you ask:

☐ Do they compare favorably to what is in the Word?

☐ Are they confirmed by other witnesses?

211

- ☐ Do they edify and build up?

- ☐ Do they bear witness to the Holy Spirit in me?

- ☐ Do they glorify God?

Do run after signs and wonders given by prophets. But don't seek a prophetic word for your own purpose or glory. Give the Spirit freedom to speak through and to you without your control or manipulation.

EXPERIENCE THE HOLY SPIRIT

Pointing to God

A prophetic sign or wonder points believers and unbelievers to God. When a prophetic word comes to you about what He is doing in the life of another person, carefully test it. Don't be so excited about a sign or wonder that you rush off to use it without first testing it. The Holy Spirit will give you prophetic words to edify and build up others. Such prophetic signs point to how the Holy Spirit is at work in your life and the lives of others.

 Write a prayer asking the Holy Spirit to speak through you prophetically as a sign of comfort and encouragement to others.

Prophetic signs given by the Spirit encourage believers to obey His Word and seek His guidance in every aspect of their walk in the Spirit.

MY DAILY WALK IN THE SPIRIT

Review today's study. Ask the Holy Spirit to give you prophetic signs that encourage and edify.

What prophetic words have been signs of encouragement to you in your walk?

_____

What prophetic words have you been given recently to encourage others?

_____

Write a prayer asking the Spirit to speak to and through you with supernatural power to edify and encourage others.

_____

Write down this week's passage to memorize.

_____

SPIRITUAL TRUTHS

- Prophetic signs and wonders are given to me and through me by the Holy Spirit to encourage and edify others.

- I need to test all prophetic words.

- Whenever a prophetic sign comes through the Spirit, I must glorify God.

Day 4: GIFTED TO HEAL

INTRODUCTION

One of the most awesome signs and miracles given by the Spirit is that of healing. The Holy Spirit empowers believers in the body with gifts of healing—physical, emotional, and spiritual. The Holy Spirit can use us as vessels of healing through which He pours His miraculous healing power.

The Holy Spirit may give someone a work of knowledge about the Spirit's healing power operating in your life. Or the Holy Spirit may choose to heal a person as you are praying for him or laying hands on him seeking God to heal.

There are a few important truths to remember as healing miracles flow from the Spirit: The Healer is always God, not the human vessel God uses. We should always seek the Healer, not just a healing miracle. Some people are so zealously seeking their healing that getting their miracle is more important to them than the Miracle Worker. Whenever healing occurs, the glory goes to God, not to the instrument God uses to heal.

EXPLORE THE WORD

God Is the One Who Heals

God heals today, just as He has healed throughout history.

📖 **Read the following scriptures, and write down what they reveal about healing.**

Exodus 15:26: _____

Psalm 103:3: _____

Psalm 107:20: _____

Psalm 147:3: _____

Isaiah 53:5; 1 Peter 2:24: _____

Jeremiah 17:14: _____

Matthew 4:24: _____

Matthew 12:15: _____

Luke 9:11: _____

Acts 5:16; 8:7: _____

1 Corinthians 12:9: _____

James 5:16: _____

EXAMINE YOURSELF

Are You Open to His Gifts of Healing?

Are you really convinced that God heals now as well as for eternity? Jesus is the same yesterday, today, and tomorrow. Just as He healed in the past, He also heals now. By the power of the Spirit, Jesus gifts believers to minister healing to others.

Answer these questions:

When was the last time you experienced the Spirit's gift of healing in your life?

_____

_____

Are you willing to pray for the healing of others? Are you willing to be used by the Spirit as a vessel of the Spirit's healing power?

_____

_____

EXPERIENCE THE HOLY SPIRIT

Who Is the Spirit Healing Now?

Are you witnessing the healing power of the Holy Spirit at work around you? Are you willing to pray in faith for the healing of others?

As I was teaching and ministering in my home congregation, one not familiar with the gifts of healing, the Spirit spoke to me about a woman being healed of tremendous pain in her legs. I spoke the word of knowledge about her healing and asked if the woman who needed that healing would stand and receive her healing from God. No one responded.

Within me rose a debate with the Spirit. I didn't want to push the issue. What if I kept announcing this healing, but no one responded? I would look foolish. After all, my reputation and integrity were at stake.

However, the Holy Spirit reminded me that only His reputation was at stake—not mine. He was the Healer, not me. It was His work of knowledge, not mine. After minutes had passed that seemed like hours to me, a woman in the back of the room slowly stood and began to walk forward to the altar. She confessed, "I knew it was me as soon as you spoke about my legs being healed, but I was afraid to stand." She was completely healed by the Holy Spirit.

Are you willing to pray for His healing and speak in faith the words of healing when He gives them—no matter what the risk?

Ask the Holy Spirit to reveal healings to you whenever He is working miracles. In your written prayer, ask that He will give you the courage and boldness to speak His miraculous healing words and to give Him the glory.

_____

MY DAILY WALK IN THE SPIRIT

Review today's study. Ask the Holy Spirit to use you as a vessel of His healing gifts.

For whose healing do you need to pray?

_____

What words of healing are you receiving from the Holy Spirit?

_____

Write a prayer asking God to heal those for whom His Spirit prompts you to pray.

_____

_____

Write down this week's passage to memorize.

_____

SPIRITUAL TRUTHS

- God heals today, just as He has healed throughout history.

- God's Spirit can gift me to speak and minister healing to others.

- I must be ready and willing to pray in the Spirit for healing whenever He prompts me to pray.

Day 5: TONGUES AS SIGNS AND WONDERS

INTRODUCTION

One of the most powerful signs given in history was the fiery tongues poured out at pentecost. Three types of tongues are mentioned in Scripture—tongues of languages unknown by the believer but understood by those with that language; tongues given for prayer and spiritual edification of the believer; and prophetic tongues and the gift of interpretation given to understand what is spoken (Acts 2; 1 Cor. 12–14).

For many Christians, the gift of tongues is a confirming manifestation or evidence of the presence of the Holy Spirit in their lives. That was the case in the household of Cornelius and among John's disciples in the early church (Acts 10; 19).

The Holy Spirit works in believers through many different signs and wonders, including speaking in tongues. You can experience this manifestation of the Spirit's presence and power if you ask. Scripture invites us to seek the spiritual gifts so that we might minister to the body. Paul's instruction was this:

> There are so many different languages in the world, and all are excellent for those who understand them, but to me they mean nothing. I will not understand people who speak those languages, and they will not understand me. Since you are so eager to have spiritual gifts, ask God for those that will be of real help to the whole church. So anyone who has the gift of speaking in tongues should pray also for the gift of interpretation in order to tell people plainly what has been said. For if I pray in tongues, my spirit is praying, but I don't understand what I am saying. Well then, what shall I do? I will do both. I will pray in the spirit, and I will pray in words I understand. I will sing in the spirit, and I will sing in words I understand. (1 COR. 14:10–15)

EXPLORE THE WORD

The Sign of Tongues

Speaking and praying in tongues are signs of the outpouring of the Holy Spirit. Not every believer has the gift of tongues, but it is available to anyone who asks.

 Read Acts 2. What happened to the early Christians when they were baptized with the Holy Spirit?

_____

 Read Acts 10 and 19. Describe the effect of the Holy Spirit upon new converts.

_____

 Read 1 Corinthians 12–14. Describe the purpose of the gift of tongues in these passages.

_____

 Read Romans 8:26. Describe how the Spirit prays through us.

_____

We should not forbid others to speak in tongues, and we can earnestly seek the gift of tongues for ourselves.

EXAMINE YOURSELF

Do I Desire This Gift?

God continues to pour out His Spirit today, just as He did that first pentecost in fulfilling the prophecy of Joel 2. Praying in tongues can draw you close in intimacy with the Holy Spirit.

If you have the gift of tongues, do you feel superior to other believers?
If you do, write a prayer of repentance.

_____

If you desire the gift of tongues, write a prayer asking the Holy Spirit for this gift.

_____

If you are judgmental and critical of people who have the gift of tongues, repent of your judgmental and critical attitude.

_____

If you pray in tongues superficially as a means to convince others or yourself of your spirituality, repent of praying vain repetitions.

_____

EXPERIENCE THE HOLY SPIRIT

Pray in the Spirit

Read 1 Corinthians 14:15 and Jude 20. As you pray, let the Holy Spirit pray through you. Don't resist how He prays through you, whether through a language you understand or one unknown to you. The key is to be open to His leading in prayer.

Pray aloud:

Jesus, baptize me with the Spirit. Pray in and through me as You desire. You have complete liberty to transform my mind, pray through my tongue, and use me as Your vessel in any way You desire. Holy Spirit, make me an instrument of Your intercession and effective prayer. Amen.

MY DAILY WALK IN THE SPIRIT

Review today's study. Ask the Holy Spirit to speak and pray through you with the gift of tongues or groanings or in any way He desires.

Describe how the Spirit prays in and through you.

_____

Repent of any hindrance you have to the Spirit praying through you.

_____

Write a prayer giving the Spirit complete liberty to pray in you.

_____

Write down what this week's passage to memorize means to you.

_____

SPIRITUAL TRUTHS

- The gift of tongues is available to me through the Spirit as a sign of His power in my life.

- I can ask for the gift of tongues.

- The Holy Spirit has liberty in my mind and mouth to pray and speak in any way He desires.

Week 10

Anointed by the Spirit for Service and Ministry

To be anointed means to be rubbed with oil or have oil poured on a person. In the Old Testament, prophets, kings, and priests were anointed with oil for service and ministry (Ex. 30; 1 Sam. 16; Num. 3:3). The symbol of oil represented the presence of the Holy Spirit to sanctify or set apart the person who was anointed for God's purposes.

Read 1 Samuel 16:13; Isaiah 61:1–2; and Luke 4:18–19.

Jesus, the Christ or Anointed One, was born of the Spirit, so we must be born of the Spirit. The Spirit of God came upon Him at baptism and then led Him into the wilderness. Jesus sent the Spirit to baptize us and to lead, teach, counsel, and comfort us. The Spirit anointed and empowered Jesus to do ministry. The Holy Spirit does the same in us—anointing and empowering us to serve God and do ministry (Acts 26:28; 1 Peter 4:16).

The apostle John wrote in 1 John 2:27 about the indwelling oil of the Spirit that teaches us all things. In the Greek, the word *anointing* is used. But here it is so interchangeable with Holy Spirit that the New Living Translation reads, "But you have received the Holy Spirit [anointing, *chrisma*], and he lives within you, so you don't need anyone to teach you what is true. For the Spirit [anointing, *chrisma*] teaches you all things, and what he teaches is true—it is not a lie. So continue in what he has taught you, and continue to live in Christ."

This oil of the Spirit is an oil of ministry, an oil of joy, an oil of holiness, and an oil prefiguring our positions of ministry in the kingdom of God as kings, priests, and prophets. This week you will discover the anointing oil of the Holy Spirit that is poured out on your life.

This Week's Passage to Memorize

As for you, the anointing you received from him remains in you, and you do not need anyone to teach you. But as his anointing teaches you about all things and as that anointing is real, not counterfeit—just as it has taught you, remain in him. (1 JOHN 2:27 NIV)

Day 1: ANOINTED AS A PRIEST

INTRODUCTION

When the priests were anointed in the Old Testament, they were set aside and separate from the other tribes of Israel. They did not own land or work outside the ministry of serving God in the tabernacle or temple. Set aside for God's service, the priests ministered to God and His people: "They were anointed and set apart to minister as priests" (Num. 3:3).

The Holy Spirit anoints you as a holy vessel to minister first to the Lord. When you don't know how to worship or serve God, He empowers you to worship and serve. When you don't know how to proclaim His Word, He teaches you the Word. In other words, the Holy Spirit equips you for priestly ministry.

The priests in the Old Testament ministered to God's people. They prepared and offered the sacrifices. They offered up prayers to God on behalf of His people as they interceded. They taught and instructed people in the law of God.

Through the work of the Holy Spirit in you, you have been anointed to be a part of a kingdom of priests. Peter wrote, "But you are not like that, for you are a chosen people. You are a kingdom of priests, God's holy nation, his very own possession. This is so you can show others the goodness of God, for he called you out of the darkness into his wonderful light" (1 Peter 2:9). As a priest of the High Priest, Jesus, you have the privilege of ushering people from the kingdom of darkness into the kingdom of light.

EXPLORE THE WORD

Minister to God and His People

An important part of the priestly ministry in the Old Testament was leading people in worship. So anointed was the worship led by the priests at the dedication of Solomon's temple that none of the worshipers could stand in God's presence. His Spirit and glory filled the temple.

> 📖 **Read 1 Chronicles 5. Describe what the priests did to lead worship.**

_____

_____

> 📖 **Describe how God's presence filled the temple.**

_____

The priests were anointed according to the Law so that they could minister to God and to God's people. That anointing set them apart as instruments of God to touch people with His power and grace. One of the most dramatic instances of how the priests ministered to people was in the cleansing of a person who had been healed of leprosy.

> 📖 **Read Leviticus 14.** What did the priest do in ministering to a healed leper when he touched the right ear, right thumb, and right toe?

_____

This anointing of the healed leper with oil and blood is a type of how the Holy Spirit ministers to us as He cleanses us from sin and prepares us to be holy unto the Lord. The blood of Christ and the oil of the Spirit cleanse the ear so that we may rightly hear and obey His voice. They cleanse the thumb, representing the work we do both in our vocation and in service to others. They cleanse the toe, representing our walk in the Spirit. Anointed as priests, we have a ministry of blood and oil to offer the cleansing power of God to sinners and see them saved, healed, and set free.

EXAMINE YOURSELF

Has the Priestly Anointing Changed You?

Everything about a priest's life was consecrated unto the Lord in Scripture. Everything! From the priest's garments to his work, daily routine, and family, everything was dedicated to the Lord. The Holy Spirit sets apart a priest to minister to the Lord and His people.

A few years ago, my wife and I were walking through the mall. We passed all kinds of people dressed in various ways. Some wore suits or dresses. Others were casually attired. And still others were immodestly dressed. Suddenly my wife grabbed my hand and squeezed it.

"What were you looking at?" she inquired as a woman in short shorts and a halter top breezed by. Admittedly that woman had caught my eye. I had allowed myself to "sneak a look." In the car driving home after our shopping trip, Judi and I had a lengthy discussion of what it meant to guard our ears and eyes, our minds and hearts so that temptation would be kept at a distance and we would remain consecrated unto the Lord.

Read the following passage from Proverbs 4:21–27. Underline the phrases in it that particularly speak to you right now in your spiritual walk.

> Don't lose sight of my words. Let them penetrate deep within your heart,
> for they bring life and radiant health to anyone who discovers their meaning.
> Above all else, guard your heart, for it affects everything you do.
> Avoid all perverse talk; stay far from corrupt speech.
> Look straight ahead, and fix your eyes on what lies before you.
> Mark out a straight path for your feet; then stick to the path and stay safe.
> Don't get sidetracked; keep your feet from following evil.

How consecrated, set apart, and holy is your life unto the Lord? On each line below, mark an *X* representing where your life is right now.

My thought life is _____
          Unholy   Holy

What I look at is _____
          Unholy   Holy

What I listen to is _____
          Unholy   Holy

My feelings are _____
          Unholy   Holy

My desires are _____
          Unholy   Holy

My work is _____
          Unholy   Holy

My walk is _____
          Unholy   Holy

Is the vessel clean through which the anointing of the Holy Spirit flows? In Exodus 40, the priests sprinkled the anointing oil on the tabernacle and everything in it so that everything was consecrated unto the Lord.

The Holy Spirit wants to anoint you as a royal priest. He desires to consecrate everything in the tabernacle of your life to His exclusive use. He is a jealous companion. He will not share His glory, power, or presence with anything or anyone else in your life. The Holy Spirit refuses to be placed in a supporting role in your life after your work, your family, your hobbies, or your desires. He takes the leading role or no role at all in you.

EXPERIENCE THE HOLY SPIRIT

Holy Unto the Lord

God very plainly says, "I, the LORD, am the one who brought you up from the land of Egypt to be your God. You must therefore be holy because I am holy" (Lev. 11:45). He has brought you out of sin and bondage into a life dedicated to Him.

Go to the Holy Spirit now. Ask Him to anoint you from head to foot with the oil of His holy presence.

Pray the following prayer, completing each sentence.

Holy Spirit, I desire as a priest ministering to the Lord and His people for You to anoint me.

Anoint my head that my thoughts _____

Anoint my ears that I may hear _____

Anoint my eyes that I may see _____

Anoint my mouth that I may speak _____

Anoint my hands that I may serve _____

Anoint my feet that I may walk _____

Anoint my life that I may live _____

Amen.

The priestly anointing does not give you a position but imparts to you the privilege of ministering to the Lord and others. As a priest, you have the privilege of worshiping and ministering, of serving and giving, of teaching and being an example of Christ in your home, church, workplace, and any other place you go. Just as a priest dressed in clergy apparel can be easily identified in a crowd, so your consecrated, priestly life can be easily identified by those around you because you are clothed and anointed in holiness.

My Daily Walk in the Spirit

📖 **Review today's study.** Let the Spirit's anointing flow over your life.

Describe how the Holy Spirit has anointed you as a priest to minister to the Lord.

_____

Describe how the Holy Spirit has anointed you as a priest to minister to His people.

_____

List anything in your life that still remains to be consecrated to the Lord's use.

_____

Ask the Holy Spirit to purify and make holy your thoughts, feelings, desires, words, and actions. Write a prayer.

_____

Write down this week's passage to memorize.

_____

Spiritual Truths

- The Holy Spirit has anointed me to be a priest in His service.

- Daily I minister to the Lord and to His people.

- Every aspect of my spiritual walk is to be dedicated, set apart, consecrated, and made holy by the Spirit.

Day 2: ANOINTED AS A KING

INTRODUCTION

Jesus is King of kings. You are a king among kings who follow Jesus. He has birthed you as royalty. Peter wrote,

> But ye are a chosen generation, a royal priesthood, an holy nation, a peculiar people; that ye should shew forth the praises of him who hath called you out of darkness into his marvellous light: Which in time past were not a people, but are now the people of God: which had not obtained mercy, but now have obtained mercy. Dearly beloved, I beseech you as strangers and pilgrims, abstain from fleshly lusts, which war against the soul; having your conversation honest among the Gentiles: that, whereas they speak against you as evildoers, they may by your good works, which they shall behold, glorify God in the day of visitation. (1 PETER 2:9–12 KJV)

Notice that as kingly priests, we are to

- show forth praises.

- abstain from worldly lusts.

- have honest conversation.

- do good works.

- be holy.

EXPLORE THE WORD

Anointed to Rule

In the Old Testament, kings were anointed to rule. As a prophet or priest poured the anointing oil over the new king, that king was set apart by God's Spirit to take charge and rule over a kingdom.

Anointed as a child of the King, Jesus, you are anointed to take back dominion over the kingdom of darkness and to rule in the kingdom of light.

📖 **Read Genesis 1:26–28.** Write down what God intended for us to rule over.

_____

In the Fall, humankind surrendered dominion to Satan and his kingdom of darkness. But through the Anointed One, Jesus the Christ, we have been delivered from darkness into light. Anointed to be a king, you are no longer to be in submission to darkness but to be a ruler in light. The anointing on Jesus was to be a Priest, King, and Prophet. That same anointing is imparted to you by the indwelling Holy Spirit.

📖 **Read Exodus 19:6 and Deuteronomy 28:9–13.** List all of the blessings that come to God's kingdom of priests.

_____

We are no longer children of darkness; we are children of light. The Holy Spirit empowers us to take back what the enemy has stolen. We are to take back dominion over the earth, transforming darkness into light.

📖 **Read Ephesians 5:1–20.** Describe the kind of life you are to live, being filled by the Spirit and walking in light.

_____

_____

_____

EXAMINE YOURSELF

Are You Ruling or Ruled?

The anointing of the Holy Spirit breaks every yoke of bondage and sets you free to be all that Christ has anointed you to be. Kings are in charge, not intimidated. Kings wearing the armor of God stand firm in the truth of God's Word. Kings are mighty prayer warriors who take the kingdom of heaven by violence. Kings refuse to submit to the enemy or his devices. Rather, kings disarm the enemy and cast him out. Are you ruling in light, or does the enemy still rule you in certain areas of your life?

Read 2 Corinthians 10:1–7. Answer these questions:

What are your weapons?_____

What war are you fighting?_____

What authority do you have? _____

What are you to conquer?_____

The King's anointing is upon you. The Anointed One has anointed you to win, not to lose; to overcome, not to surrender to the world; to be victorious, not to be defeated.

List the areas in your life where you need to claim victory over darkness.

_____

EXPERIENCE THE HOLY SPIRIT

Armed and Dangerous

As a king, you have been given armor to wear. You do not march into battle defenseless. You have the armor of God.

Ask the Holy Spirit to pour out His oil of anointing upon you as a king wearing the armor of God.

Read Ephesians 6:10–18. Pray the following prayer adapted from this passage.

Lord Jesus, by the Spirit's anointing, make me strong with Your mighty power. Spirit of God, help me put on all of God's armor so that I will be able to stand firm against all strategies and tricks of the devil.

Holy Spirit, help me understand that I am not fighting against people made of flesh and blood, but against the evil rulers and authorities of the unseen world, against those mighty powers of darkness who rule this world, and against wicked spirits in the heavenly realms.

Empower me to use every piece of God's armor to resist the enemy in the time of evil, so that after the battle I will still be standing firm. Help me to stand my ground, putting on the sturdy belt of truth and the body armor of God's righteousness.

Spirit of God, put on me the shoes of peace that come from the good news, so that I will be fully prepared.

In every battle strengthen my faith as my shield to stop the fiery arrows aimed at me by Satan. Anoint me, Holy Spirit, with the helmet of salvation; put in my hand Your sword, Holy Spirit, which is the Word of God.

Spirit of God, pray through me at all times and on every occasion in Your mighty power. Equip me to stay alert and be persistent in my prayers for all Christians everywhere. Amen.

In the power of the Holy Spirit, you will be anointed to fulfill Christ's commission to you as both a priest and a king: "And I have given you authority over all the power of the enemy, and you can walk among snakes and scorpions and crush them. Nothing will injure you. But don't rejoice just because evil spirits obey you; rejoice because your names are registered as citizens of heaven" (Luke 10:19–20).

My Daily Walk in the Spirit

📖 **Review today's study.** Walk in the authority of the King's anointing on your life.

Describe the battles in which you presently find yourself.

_____

Now describe how the Holy Spirit is anointing you as a king to win those battles.

_____

Write a prayer thanking God's Spirit for the armor to win the battles.

_____

Write down this week's passage to memorize.

_____

Spiritual Truths

- Anointed as a king, I have been destined to win the battles and overcome the world.

- Now is the time for me to take back dominion through the Spirit's anointing.

- I have the armor of God for standing firm in every battle.

Day 3: ANOINTED AS A PROPHET

INTRODUCTION

In the Old Testament, God took the prophetic anointing that was on Moses and put it on seventy leaders of Israel. Scripture affirms that in all of Israel there was not a prophet like Moses (Deut. 34:10). God's Spirit took the prophetic anointing or mantle that was on Moses and empowered those seventy to prophesy.

📖 **Read Numbers 11:25–29.**

Jesus was anointed by God's Spirit as a prophet both to Israel and to the Gentiles. He spoke God's Word announcing the kingdom of God. The prophet is a mouthpiece of God's Word to His people. You are anointed as a prophet to speak God's Word to your family, church, workplace, and world. With the anointing that is now on your life through Christ Jesus, you must boldly proclaim His truth. The mark of a prophet is that he will live to please God, not man; to speak God's Word, not man's; to proclaim truth in the midst of the world's lies.

EXPLORE THE WORD

The Prophet's Anointing

In 2 Kings 2, Elisha desired to receive the prophetic anointing that was on Elijah's life. He followed Elijah and served him until the time came for him to receive a double portion of the anointing on Elijah's life.

Read 2 Kings 2. Describe the anointing that was passed from Elijah to Elisha.

_____

Reread Numbers 11:25. Describe what happened when the prophetic anointing passed from Moses to the seventy.

_____

Read 1 Corinthians 14. Describe how the gift of prophecy empowered by the Holy Spirit ministers in the church.

_____

The prophetic anointing may come upon your life to minister to another believer or the church. That anointing carries with it a tremendous responsibility to hear God and then to obey faithfully what He says.

EXAMINE YOURSELF

Are You Listening . . . Are You Prophesying . . . Are You Obeying?
The Holy Spirit will anoint you to prophesy in order to edify others. But before you can prophesy, you must hear the Spirit's voice.

What is the Holy Spirit speaking to you?

_____

_____

At times, the Spirit will prophetically speak into your life to have you pray. He may not release you to share what He has said, only to pray and intercede. The Holy Spirit will reveal deep things to you so that you may pray the Father's heart and see His will done on earth as it is in heaven.

What is the Holy Spirit prophetically revealing to you so that you can pray and intercede for the saints and His church?

_____

_____

At other times, the Holy Spirit will prophetically speak to you and tell you to share what He says with another believer or with the body of Christ. He never speaks to judge, but He will edify, comfort, counsel, convict, and correct.

Describe a time when the Holy Spirit gave you a prophetic word for another believer or the church.

_____

_____

What will keep you from obeying the Spirit when He prophetically speaks to you?

_____

_____

In the book of Acts, the apostles and early believers were constantly speaking prophetically to the Jewish leaders about Jesus the Messiah. The prophetic anointing on their lives often resulted in persecution. Are you willing to speak obediently God's Word to others even if it means persecution and rejection?

EXPERIENCE THE HOLY SPIRIT

Let the Spirit Anoint You to Speak

Take time each day to listen to the Spirit's voice, especially as He speaks to you through these ways (check the ways you most often hear His voice):

☐ The Bible   ☐ Worship

☐ Prayer   ☐ Being still before Him

☐ The counsel of   ☐ Other: _____
    other believers

Take at least fifteen to thirty minutes to be still before God. Read the Word. Pray. Be silent and listen. Ask for the prophetic anointing that was on Jesus to rest upon your life. Listen to the Spirit's voice.

Write down what the Spirit is prophetically revealing to you right now.

_____

_____

Never use what the Spirit gives you to control, intimidate, dominate, or manipulate others. Likewise, don't let the prophetic words spoken to you be controlling, intimidating, dominating, manipulating, or legalistic. Test all prophecies with the Word of God, the witness of the Spirit, and the counsel of other believers.

When the Holy Spirit gives you a word to share with the church or others, submit that word to one in spiritual authority over you. Let that word be tested (1 Thess. 5:20–21) and confirmed by others who are filled with the Holy Spirit. When you have been released by the Spirit and those in spiritual authority, share the word you have received in love and grace.

My Daily Walk in the Spirit

Review today's study. Listen to the voice of the Holy Spirit.

Write down the prophetic words that have been spoken to you and that have been fulfilled.

_____

Write down what the Spirit is prophetically revealing to you for prayer today for your family, church, or colleagues at work or school.

_____

Write down any word He is giving you to speak to the church or other believers.

_____

Ask the Holy Spirit to anoint you with His Spirit to be a bold prophet proclaiming His Word and truth.

_____

Spiritual Truths

- I am anointed as a prophet to speak the truth of God's Word.

- I can hear the Spirit's voice as He speaks prophetically into my life.

- I need to test all prophecies and to pray and speak as the Spirit leads.

Day 4: ANOINTED TO MINISTER

INTRODUCTION

When the Anointed One stood before the synagogue in Nazareth, Jesus read from the Isaiah scroll. The passage He chose to read from Isaiah 61 defined His ministry and all those who would walk after Him in His anointing.

Carefully read this passage from Isaiah:

> The Spirit of the Sovereign LORD is upon me, because the LORD has appointed me to bring good news to the poor. He has sent me to comfort the broken-hearted and to announce that captives will be released and prisoners will be freed. He has sent me to tell those who mourn that the time of the LORD's favor has come, and with it, the day of God's anger against their enemies. To all who mourn in Israel, he will give beauty for ashes, joy instead of mourning, praise instead of despair. For the LORD has planted them like strong and graceful oaks for his own glory. They will rebuild the ancient ruins, repairing cities long ago destroyed. They will revive them, though they have been empty for many generations. Foreigners will be your servants. They will feed your flocks and plow your fields and tend your vineyards. You will be called priests of the LORD, ministers of our God. You will be fed with the treasures of the nations and will boast in their riches. (ISA. 61:1–6)

Today we will explore how the anointing on Jesus now lives in you as a "little anointed one" or Christian. Anointed as Priest, King, and Prophet, Jesus entered into ministry. Likewise, the Spirit anoints you to minister in the same way that Jesus did.

EXPLORE THE WORD

For What Ministry Are You Anointed?

Here is the fourfold anointing to minister:

1. Bring good news to the poor.

2. Comfort the brokenhearted.

3. Announce that captives will be released and prisoners freed.

4. Tell those who mourn that the time of God's favor has arrived and, with it, the day of God's anger against their enemies.

Reread Isaiah 61:1–6. Answer these questions:

What is the good news you bring to the poor (Matt. 25; John 10:1–10)?

_____

Who are the brokenhearted (Matt. 5:1–16)?

_____

What captives and prisoners need to be released (Luke 4:40–44)?

_____

What is the favor of God (Matt. 11:1–6)?

_____

_____

EXAMINE YOURSELF

Where Are You Ministering in Christ's Anointing?

The Spirit of the Lord has anointed you to minister in Jesus' name. That ministry is one not of position but of service. You have been called to serve with the attitude of servanthood (Phil. 2).

As you serve, you will be empowered by the anointing of the Spirit to obey whatever Jesus wants you to say and do.

📖 **Describe how you are proclaiming good news to others.**

_____

📖 **Describe how you are comforting the brokenhearted.**

_____

📖 **Describe how you are ministering to those who are in bondage.**

_____

📖 **Describe where you see the favor of God blessing others through your ministry.**

_____

EXPERIENCE THE HOLY SPIRIT

When Will You Step Out?

Often the anointing comes after you have stepped out in faith. Some people never get around to ministry because they are always waiting around for the anointing. My friend, you can stop waiting around. You do not need to fall in the Spirit, shake under the power of God, or have a dramatic prophetic revelation to minister. The anointing to minister already resides in you through the indwelling Holy Spirit. You have the commission, calling, and power to minister. Just do it!

What often keeps us from ministering is not the lack of anointing but the lack of faith. We are powerless to minister because we spend too little time in His presence.

📖 **List anything that keeps you from ministering in Jesus' anointing power.**

_____

📖 **Ask the Holy Spirit to remove every hindrance and to fill you with the boldness to minister according to Isaiah 61.**

_____

We often ask, "Who is waiting on the other side of your obedience?" You have the anointing, but do you have the courage to obey? Christ's anointing in you and on you is not a badge of identity; it is an empowerment to walk powerfully in ministry.

My Daily Walk in the Spirit

📖 **Review today's study.** Minister today in Christ's anointing.

List brokenhearted persons whom the Holy Spirit is leading you to comfort.

_____

List imprisoned persons to whom the Holy Spirit is leading you to take the good news of deliverance.

_____

List persons poor in body or spirit to whom the Spirit is calling you to serve.

_____

Write a prayer asking for boldness to minister in Jesus' name.

_____

Write down this week's passage to memorize.

_____

Spiritual Truths

- The anointing of Christ on my life empowers me to minister in His name.

- I must obey His call to minister to the poor, brokenhearted, and captives.

- The Holy Spirit will give me the boldness and compassion I need to minister to others.

Day 5: ANOINTED FOR HOLINESS

INTRODUCTION

The Holy Spirit's anointing is on your life to teach you truth so that you will live a holy life. John wrote,

> But you have received the Holy Spirit [the anointing], and he lives within you, so you don't need anyone to teach you what is true. For the Spirit teaches you all things, and what he teaches is true—it is not a lie. So continue in what he has taught you, and continue to live in Christ. And now, dear children, continue to live in fellowship with Christ so that when he returns, you will be full of courage and not shrink back from him in shame. Since we know that God is always right, we also know that all who do what is right are his children. (1 JOHN 2:27–29)

The Spirit's anointing on you empowers you to boldly live the Christian life. The Spirit sanctifies and makes you holy so that you can minister effectively to lost and hurting people in the world. It's God's will for His Spirit to make you holy.

EXPLORE THE WORD

God's Will—Your Holiness

God's will for you is that you live a pure and holy life, giving glory to Him. The anointing on your life is the oil for the flame burning brightly in you. You are a light dispelling darkness. You are a fire consuming evil. You are a beacon in the night. You are pure in the midst of impurity.

📖 **Read 1 Thessalonians 4:1–8.** Describe the holy life that God wills for you to live.

_____

_____

As you live a holy life, the anointing of Christ flows through you and touches those around you. Through you flow the good news of salvation, the healing power of Christ, and the deliverance power to set others free from bondage. It is not you but the Spirit in you who empowers you to be holy.

EXAMINE YOURSELF

Are You Anointed?

The Spirit's anointing is not only for some Christians. Perhaps you have heard some say, "Oh, he's anointed to preach," or "She's anointed to prophesy." The truth is that the same anointing that was in Christ is in all His followers. Some obediently walk in that anointing. Others seem to hide the anointing. Why? Perhaps it's fear of losing control or doing something that might feel uncomfortable.

📖 **What unholy areas of your life keep the anointing hidden from others?**

_____

_____

Often I blame others for not seeing Jesus in me when in truth, they don't see His anointing on my life because I am hindering the Spirit. More often than not, I am the problem, not them.

📖 **What's in you that must get out so that others can see Jesus through you?**

_____

_____

EXPERIENCE THE HOLY SPIRIT

Walk in Anointed Holiness

The priests in the Old Testament had holy anointing oil: "Say to the people of Israel, 'This will always be my holy anointing oil. It must never be poured on the body of an ordinary person, and you must never make any of it for yourselves. It is holy, and you must treat it as holy'" (Ex. 30:31–32). Guess what? You are not an ordinary person. You have died to self and are quickened or brought to life by the Holy Spirit as a new creation.

The Holy Spirit wants to pour His holy oil on your life. Have you become complacent about the anointing on your life? Has your spiritual walk grown routine or even stale? You can walk in anointed holiness. What you need is fresh oil. The psalmist proclaimed, "I shall be anointed with fresh oil" (Ps. 92:10 KJV).

📖 **Write a prayer asking the Holy Spirit to anoint you with fresh oil.**

_____

His fresh oil renews your boldness, makes holy your walk, empowers your ministry, and flows right through you as a healing and saving balm for others.

My Daily Walk in the Spirit

📖 **Review today's study.** Walk in the Spirit's holiness.

Repent of the unholiness in your life.

_____

Ask Jesus to forgive and cleanse your life by the Spirit.

_____

Write a prayer for fresh oil to be poured on your life.

_____

What has the passage to memorize meant to you this week?

_____

How is the Holy Spirit using you in ministry?

_____

Spiritual Truths

- God's Spirit wills for me to be holy.

- I need to repent of the areas of my life that keep others from seeing Christ's anointing on my life.

- I can receive fresh oil from the Spirit whenever I ask.

Part 4

Walk in the Spirit

Week 11

PRAYING IN THE SPIRIT

Scripture commands, "Continue to pray as you are directed by the Holy Spirit" (Jude 20). The Holy Spirit directs and guides our prayers so that we know what and how to pray. Paul wrote, "The Holy Spirit helps us in our distress. For we don't even know what we should pray for, nor how we should pray. But the Holy Spirit prays for us with groanings that cannot be expressed in words. And the Father who knows all hearts knows what the Spirit is saying, for the Spirit pleads for us believers in harmony with God's own will" (Rom. 8:26–27).

For the first ten weeks of *Experiencing the Holy Spirit,* you placed a strong emphasis on exploring the Word. You studied what the Word reveals about the person and work of the Holy Spirit. Then you spent time in examining yourself. You lined up your life against the Word and asked the Holy Spirit to reveal what is inside you. Finally you opened yourself up to the work of the Holy Spirit in your life through experiencing the Holy Spirit. In that time with the Spirit, you asked for the Holy Spirit to speak to you, teach you, and guide you in His ways.

In the last section of this workbook, you will go deeper into the Spirit as you pray and walk daily in the Spirit. We might say that the first ten weeks were a time of being discipled and practicing the discipline of a spiritual walk. These last two weeks are times of application.

During this week, you will pray in the Spirit. Praying in the Spirit involves:

- Speaking and praying the Word.

- Listening to the Spirit.

- Obeying the Spirit.

The Holy Spirit speaks to us primarily through the Word. Scripture is Spirit-breathed for our instruction and correction: "All Scripture is inspired by God ['Spirit breathed' literally in the Greek] and is useful to teach us what is true and to make us realize what is wrong in our lives. It straightens us out and teaches us to do what is right. It is God's way of preparing us in every way, fully equipped for every good thing God wants us to do" (2 Tim. 3:16–17).

Each day of this week will focus on a few scriptures for you to speak and pray in a particular aspect of your prayer life. These scriptures are personalized so that you can apply them directly to your life and circumstances. Then reflection questions will be asked to direct you in listening to the Holy Spirit. Finally you will write down what the Holy Spirit is instructing you to do in obedience.

To remind you once again of the work of the Spirit, read aloud this passage daily during the week:

> But it is actually best for you that I go away, because if I don't, the Counselor won't come. If I do go away, he will come because I will send him to you. And when he comes, he will convince the world of its sin, and of God's righteousness, and of the coming judgment. The world's sin is unbelief in me. Righteousness is available because I go to the Father, and you will see me no more. Judgment will come because the prince of this world has already been judged. Oh, there is so much more I want to tell you, but you can't bear it now. When the Spirit of truth comes, he will guide you into all truth. He will not be presenting his own ideas; he will be telling you what he has heard. He will tell you about the future. He will bring me glory by revealing to you whatever he receives from me. All that the Father has is mine; this is what I mean when I say that the Spirit will reveal to you whatever he receives from me. In just a little while I will be gone, and you won't see me anymore. Then, just a little while after that, you will see me again. (JOHN 16:7–16)

Day 1: STAYING REPENTANT BEFORE THE SPIRIT

INTRODUCTION

The sin in us keeps us from praying righteously or effectively. Praying in the Spirit begins with asking the Holy Spirit to do His work of conviction in our lives. Paul wrote,

> God can use sorrow in our lives to help us turn away from sin and seek salvation. We will never regret that kind of sorrow. But sorrow without repentance is the kind that results in death. Just see what this godly sorrow produced in you! Such earnestness, such concern to clear yourselves, such indignation, such alarm, such longing to see me, such zeal, and such a readiness to punish the wrongdoer. You showed that you have done everything you could to make things right. (2 Cor. 7:10–11)

You know areas in your life that may be strongholds right now (2 Cor. 10). You need to repent of the areas, confessing the sinful habit in thought or action to Christ. Remember this promise and warning: "If we confess our sins to him, he is faithful and just to forgive us and to cleanse us from every wrong. If we claim we have not sinned, we are calling God a liar and showing that his word has no place in our hearts" (1 John 1:9–10).

SPEAK AND PRAY THE WORD

Praying Psalm 51

David's prayer of repentance is the best place to start as you confess your sins before God. Take the steps noted at the top of the next page.

- Become quiet before God.

- Ask the Spirit to reveal to you any hidden sins that do not immediately come to mind.

- Pray this adapted prayer from Psalm 51, and insert your sins in the space provided.

Have mercy on me, O God, because of Your unfailing love. Because of Your great compassion, blot out the stain of my sins, which are

_____

_____

Wash me clean from my guilt. Purify me from my sin. For I recognize my shameful deeds—they haunt me day and night. Against You, and You alone, have I sinned; I have done what is evil in Your sight. You will be proved right in what You say, and Your judgment against me is just. For I was born a sinner—yes, from the moment my mother conceived me. But You desire honesty from the heart, so You can teach me to be wise in my inmost being. Purify me from my sins, and I will be clean; wash me, and I will be whiter than snow. Oh, give me back my joy again; You have broken me—now let me rejoice. Don't keep looking at my sins. Remove the stain of my guilt. Create in me a clean heart, O God. Renew a right spirit within me. Do not banish me from Your presence, and don't take Your Holy Spirit from me. Restore to me again the joy of Your salvation, and make me willing to obey You. Amen.

Thank the Lord for His shed blood that washes away all sin. Sing a chorus or hymn of thanksgiving.

LISTEN TO THE SPIRIT

Be Still and Listen

Be still before God for at least twenty minutes. Listen to the voice of the Spirit.

Write down whatever He reveals to you about how to stay pure and holy from the sins you have just confessed.

OBEY THE SPIRIT

No Excuses

Do not make excuses for your unwillingness to obey because of lack of time, busyness, or weakness. The Holy Spirit has empowered you to obey whatever He asks. Simply surrender.

 Write down the thoughts you will think and the actions you will take to obey what the Holy Spirit has commanded you to do.

 Write a prayer asking the Holy Spirit for a person with whom you can confess your sins according to James 5:16, "Confess your sins to each other."

The pious fellowship permits no one to be a sinner. So everyone must conceal his sin from himself and from the fellowship. We dare not be sinners. Many Christians are unthinkably horrified when a real sinner is suddenly discovered among the righteous. So we remain alone with our sin, living in lies and hypocrisy. The fact is that we are sinners!

—Dietrich Bonhoeffer, from *Life Together*

Day 2: PRAYING PRAISE AND ADORATION

INTRODUCTION

After being filled with the Spirit, you will "sing psalms and hymns and spiritual songs among yourselves, making music to the Lord in your hearts. And you will always give thanks for everything to God the Father in the name of our Lord Jesus Christ" (Eph. 5:19–20).

Praying in the Spirit sings praises and thanksgiving to the Lord. Praying in the Spirit releases heartfelt adoration to Jesus. You can join the choruses in heaven by singing your praise to Jesus both in your natural language and in your spiritual language (1 Cor. 12).

SPEAK AND PRAY THE WORD

Praying the Choruses of Heaven

You may know a melody or create a new song based on the praises of heaven. Pray and sing the Word:

> You are worthy to take the scroll and break its seals and open it.
> For you were killed, and your blood has ransomed people for God
>   from every tribe and language and people and nation.
> And you have caused them to become God's kingdom and his priests.
> And they will reign on the earth. (Rev. 5:9–10)

> The Lamb is worthy—the Lamb who was killed.
>   He is worthy to receive power and riches
>   and wisdom and strength
>   and honor and glory and blessing. (Rev. 5:12)

Blessing and honor and glory and power
    belong to the one sitting on the throne
    and to the Lamb forever and ever. (Rev. 5:13)

Amen! Blessing and glory and wisdom
    and thanksgiving and honor and power and strength
    belong to our God forever and forever. Amen! (Rev. 7:12)

LISTEN TO THE SPIRIT

Let the Spirit Teach You a New Song

The Holy Spirit will fill you with His new songs of praise and adoration. He will teach you spiritual songs to sing in worshiping Jesus. Psalm 149:1 instructs,

> Praise the LORD!
> Sing to the LORD a new song.
> Sing his praises in the assembly of the faithful.

Paul wrote, "Well then, what shall I do? I will do both. I will pray in the spirit, and I will pray in words I understand. I will sing in the spirit, and I will sing in words I understand" (1 Cor. 14:15).

Spend at least twenty minutes listening to the Holy Spirit. Ask Him to teach you new songs of praise and adoration. Write down and then sing a new song He gives you.

_____

_____

_____

OBEY THE SPIRIT

Adore Jesus

The Holy Spirit will reveal when and where He wants you to sing praises to and adore Jesus. You may need to set aside your travel time in the car or your TV time in the evening to worship Jesus.

 Ask the Holy Spirit to tell you when to praise and adore Jesus in your daily schedule. Write down His instructions.

_____

_____

We never really adore Him, until we arrive at the moment when we worship Him for what He is in Himself apart from any consideration of the impact of His Divine Selfhood upon our desires and our welfare. Then we adore Him, regardless of whether any personal benefit is in anticipation or not.

—Albert E. Day, from *An Autobiography*

Day 3: THE SPIRIT INTERCEDING THROUGH US

INTRODUCTION

How much doesn't happen because we are reluctant to pray? Jesus commanded us to pray God's will in heaven down to earth. Our lack of intercession hinders the kingdom of God on earth; it's that simple and tragic!

- Who isn't getting saved right now because we are not praying?

- Who isn't being healed right now because we fail to pray?

- Who isn't being set free right now because we are not allowing the Spirit to intercede through us?

Paul reminded us, "The Holy Spirit helps us in our distress. For we don't even know what we should pray for, nor how we should pray. But the Holy Spirit prays for us with groanings that cannot be expressed in words. And the Father who knows all hearts knows what the Spirit is saying, for the Spirit pleads for us believers in harmony with God's own will" (Rom. 8:26–27).

SPEAK AND PRAY THE WORD

Praying As Daniel Prayed

When praying for others, you might begin with Daniel's intercession for God's people from Daniel 9.

Pray the intercessory prayer adapted from Daniel 9, which appears on the next page.

O Lord, You are a great and awesome God! You always fulfill Your promises of unfailing love to those who love You and keep Your commands. But we have sinned and done wrong. We have rebelled against You and scorned Your commands and regulations.

We have refused to listen to Your servants the prophets, who spoke Your messages to our kings and princes and ancestors and to all the people of the land. Lord, You are in the right; but our faces are covered with shame, just as You see us now . . . In view of all Your faithful mercies, Lord, please turn Your furious anger away from us. O our God, hear Your servant's prayer! Listen as I plead. For Your own sake, Lord, smile again on Your desolate sanctuary. O my God, listen to me and hear my request. Open Your eyes and see our wretchedness . . . We do not ask because we deserve help, but because You are so merciful. O Lord, hear. O Lord, forgive. O Lord, listen and act! For Your own sake, O my God, do not delay, for Your people bear Your name.

Claim God's promise in intercession: "Then if my people who are called by my name will humble themselves and pray and seek my face and turn from their wicked ways, I will hear from heaven and will forgive their sins and heal their land" (2 Chron. 7:14).

LISTEN TO THE SPIRIT

For Whom and About What Are You to Intercede?

God said, "I sought for a man among them, that should make up the hedge, and stand in the gap before me for the land, that I should not destroy it: but I found none" (Ezek. 22:30 KJV). God's Spirit is looking for intercessors to stand in the gap for His people and the church. Are you willing to intercede?

Listen to the Spirit. For whom is He telling you to intercede? List their names.

_____

What is He telling you to pray? Write down what the Spirit is speaking to you.

_____

OBEY THE SPIRIT

When Will You Pray?

God's Word commands, "Pray at all times and on every occasion in the power of the Holy Spirit. Stay alert and be persistent in your prayers for all Christians everywhere" (Eph. 6:18). Make a commitment to pray in the Spirit daily for others. Make intercession part of your prayer discipline.

Write down when the Spirit desires for you to intercede daily.

_____

Let us each find out what the work is, and who the souls are entrusted to our special prayers; let us make our intercession for them our life of fellowship with God, and we shall not only find the promises of power in prayer made true to us, but we shall then first begin to realize how our abiding in Christ and His abiding in us make us share in His own joy of blessing and saving men.

—Andrew Murray, from *With Christ in the School of Prayer*

Day 4: Praying Our Petitions

Introduction

We pray for our needs. Our needs arise out of our desire to serve Him, not our desire to acquire or obtain. To pray for our needs responds to Jesus' invitation:

> And so I tell you, keep on asking, and you will be given what you ask for. Keep on looking, and you will find. Keep on knocking, and the door will be opened. For everyone who asks, receives. Everyone who seeks, finds. And the door is opened to everyone who knocks. You fathers—if your children ask for a fish, do you give them a snake instead? Or if they ask for an egg, do you give them a scorpion? Of course not! If you sinful people know how to give good gifts to your children, how much more will your heavenly Father give the Holy Spirit to those who ask him. (LUKE 11:9–13)

Speak and Pray the Word

Praying As Jesus Taught

As you begin to pray for your needs, petition as Jesus taught:

> Our Father in heaven, may your name be honored. May your Kingdom come soon. May your will be done here on earth, just as it is in heaven. Give us our food for today, and forgive us our sins, just as we have forgiven those who have sinned against us. And don't let us yield to temptation, but deliver us from the evil one. (MATT. 6:9–13)

LISTEN TO THE SPIRIT

What Does the Spirit Say You Need?

Not trusting my flesh or soul to know truly what I need, I must rely on the revelation of the Holy Spirit. Only He knows my needs. I tend to get in the way of His revelation.

When I pray asking for my needs, I must listen to the Spirit. He knows me better than I know myself. I invite you to follow these steps:

1. Ask the Holy Spirit to reveal your needs to you. Write them down.

_____

2. Ask the Holy Spirit to crucify your wants. Write down what He says.

_____

3. Ask the Holy Spirit to fill you with His desires. Write down what He wills for you.

_____

OBEY THE SPIRIT

What Do You Need to Surrender?

Too often we waste our time praying vain repetitions for needs we do not have. And we hold on to feelings, thoughts, and desires that distract us from our real needs.

Write down the "wants" the Spirit has told you to surrender.

_____

Grant me, O Lord, heavenly wisdom,
that I may learn to seek you above all things,
and to understand all other things as they are
according to the order of your wisdom. Amen.

—Thomas à Kempis

Day 5: The Spirit Praying Through Us

Introduction

Earlier this week we read from Romans 8:26–27 that the Holy Spirit prays through us when we do not know how to pray. Instead of filling the silence with words, we need to be still and listen to the Spirit's voice.

- He can pray through us using our prayer language.

- He can pray through us when we are silent.

- He can pray through us in groans and utterances beyond words.

The only issue is this: Are we willing to remain silent and still?

Speak and Pray the Word

Being Still

Pray these prayers adapted from the Word:

> Lord, I will be still in Your presence and wait patiently for You to act. I will not worry about evil people who prosper or fret about their wicked schemes. Amen. (See Ps. 37:7.)

> Listen to my voice in the morning, Lord. Each morning I bring my requests to You and wait expectantly. Amen. (See Ps. 5:3.)

> I wait quietly before You, O God, for my salvation comes from You. You alone are my rock and my salvation, my fortress where I will never be shaken. Amen. (See Ps. 62:1–2.)

LISTEN TO THE SPIRIT

What Is He Saying Out of the Stillness?

If the Spirit is to speak so that you can hear Him, then you must silently wait upon Him.

Sit quietly and silently before the Lord. Listen to the Spirit's voice. Write down whatever He speaks to you in the silence, and then go to the Word and find the passages that confirm what He is saying. If the Word does not confirm what you hear, the Spirit is not speaking.

_____

_____

_____

OBEY THE SPIRIT

How Hard Is It for You to Be Still?

Turn off the tapes and the music. Silence the noises around you. Lie down or sit or walk in silence. Hear His voice.

If you cannot be still, write a prayer asking the Spirit to teach you the discipline of silence.

_____

_____

_____

But to the man who withdraws himself from all that is of world and man, and prepares to wait upon God alone, the Father will reveal himself . . . The secrecy of the inner chamber and the closed door, the entire separation from all around us, is an image of, and so a help to that inner spiritual sanctuary, the secret of God's tabernacle, within the veil, where our spirit truly comes into contact with the Invisible One.

—Andrew Murray, from *With Christ in the School of Prayer*

Week 12

LIVING IN THE SPIRIT

Walking in the Spirit involves us body and soul. Our thoughts, feelings, decisions, desires, and actions all come under the control and direction of the Holy Spirit.

In this final week, you will evaluate the areas of your life that need to be fully surrendered to the Holy Spirit. You are not in control; He is.

Each day you will read a text and then ask the Holy Spirit to use the Word as a sharp sword revealing your walk with Him. Hebrews 4:12–13 states, "For the word of God is full of living power. It is sharper than the sharpest knife, cutting deep into our innermost thoughts and desires. It exposes us for what we really are. Nothing in all creation can hide from him. Everything is naked and exposed before his eyes. This is the God to whom we must explain all that we have done."

Each day you will

- examine your life according to the Word and Spirit.

- ask the Spirit for guidance and direction.

- obey the Spirit.

You must be open to the Spirit's conviction at all times. He uses the Word as a scalpel to do spiritual surgery on your life. As you daily walk in the Spirit, He exposes any misstep in your walk by His Word.

Memorize This Verse

> If we are living now by the Holy Spirit, let us follow the Holy Spirit's leading
> in every part of our lives. (GAL. 5:25)

Day 1: THE WALK OF LOVE

INTRODUCTION

Jesus made it abundantly clear that others will know us by our love: "So now I am giving you a new commandment: Love each other. Just as I have loved you, you should love each other. Your love for one another will prove to the world that you are my disciples" (John 13:34–35).

Of course, love is a fruit of the Spirit (Gal. 5:22), so your daily walk will reflect love for God, others, and self.

EXAMINE YOURSELF

How Deep Is Your Love?
Take a true-false test on love:

__ I love my enemies.	__ I love unconditionally.
__ I love those who persecute me.	__ I love the Lord with my whole heart, mind, soul, and strength.
__ I love patiently.	__ I love my neighbor.
__ I love without expecting to be loved in return.	__ I love myself.

Were there more true than false answers? Read 1 Corinthians 13. Ask the Holy Spirit to reveal any area of your love life that needs to be strengthened or corrected.

📖 Write down what the Holy Spirit has revealed to you.

_____

ASK THE HOLY SPIRIT FOR GUIDANCE AND DIRECTION

The Spirit Commands Us to Love

📖 Who is the Holy Spirit asking you to love?

_____

📖 How does He want you to show your love?

_____

📖 With whom have you been offended, and how do you need to show love to them?

_____

OBEY THE SPIRIT

Demonstrate Love

📖 In what new ways does the Holy Spirit want you to demonstrate God's love in your daily walk with Him?

_____

Day 2: Don't Walk According to Your Sinful Desires

Introduction

Walking in the Spirit involves avoiding certain attitudes, behaviors, and people. Psalm 1 declares, "Oh, the joys of those who do not follow the advice of the wicked, or stand around with sinners, or join in with scoffers" (v. 1). The Holy Spirit empowers you to avoid the desires of your sinful self. You can die to your desires and live to God.

Examine Yourself

Sins of the Flesh

Paul gave a detailed description in Galatians 5 of all the sins of the flesh that keep us from walking in the Spirit.

In the text from Galatians, circle all the sins that the Holy Spirit is revealing to you that are in your walk.

I advise you to live according to your new life in the Holy Spirit. Then you won't be doing what your sinful nature craves. The old sinful nature loves to do evil, which is just opposite from what the Holy Spirit wants. And the Spirit gives us desires that are opposite from what the sinful nature desires. These two forces are constantly fighting each other, and your choices are never free from this conflict. But when you are directed by the Holy Spirit, you are no longer subject to the law. When you follow the desires of your sinful nature, your lives will produce these evil results: sexual immorality, impure thoughts, eagerness for lustful pleasure, idolatry, participation in demonic activities, hostility, quarreling, jealousy, outbursts of anger, selfish ambition, divisions, the feeling that everyone is wrong except those in your own little group, envy, drunkenness, wild parties, and other kinds of sin. Let me tell you again, as I have before, that anyone living that sort of life will not inherit the Kingdom of God. (GAL. 5:16–21)

ASK THE HOLY SPIRIT FOR GUIDANCE AND DIRECTION

What Is the Holy Spirit Telling You to Stop Doing?

Describe what the Holy Spirit is telling you about the sinful desires in your life.

_____

OBEY THE SPIRIT

The Spirit Guides

The Holy Spirit not only convicts; He guides you in how to stop following the desires of your flesh.

Describe how you will obey the Spirit in not walking according to your sinful desires.

_____

Day 3: MINISTER IN THE POWER OF THE HOLY SPIRIT

INTRODUCTION

As we discussed early in this study, the Holy Spirit moved mightily in the early church. He demonstrated His power through miracles, signs, wonders, salvations, healings, boldness, answered prayer, and many other ways.

Are you seeing the manifestation of this power in your life?

EXAMINE YOURSELF

Empowered by the Spirit

Read the following passage from Acts. Underline every evidence of the Spirit's power you see in the early church, and then circle the evidences of power that you see in your own life.

> Those who believed what Peter said were baptized and added to the church— about three thousand in all. They joined with the other believers and devoted themselves to the apostles' teaching and fellowship, sharing in the Lord's Supper and in prayer. A deep sense of awe came over them all, and the apostles performed many miraculous signs and wonders. And all the believers met together constantly and shared everything they had. They sold their possessions and shared the proceeds with those in need. They worshiped together at the Temple each day, met in homes for the Lord's Supper, and shared their meals with great joy and generosity—all the while praising God and enjoying the goodwill of all the people. And each day the Lord added to their group those who were being saved. (ACTS 2:41–47)

ASK THE HOLY SPIRIT FOR GUIDANCE AND DIRECTION

Are You Living in the Power of the Spirit?

The baptism of the Holy Spirit comes in power. How is His power being manifested in your life?

Write down where the Holy Spirit manifests His power in you daily.

_____

Write down where you have seen the Spirit's power in your life during the last three months.

_____

OBEY THE SPIRIT

Where Do You Need the Power?

Every Christian needs more power from the Holy Spirit in certain areas of his life. We are always growing. Where does the Holy Spirit need to anoint you in power today?

Write down what the Holy Spirit reveals to you.

_____

Will you surrender to His power?

Day 4: OBEYING THE CALL

INTRODUCTION

Jesus commissions us to obey His call to go into all the world and to operate in the power of the Holy Spirit. Are you obeying the call to the world or hanging out in your home and at church? Either the Spirit has empowered you to go out in the name of Jesus, or He isn't the driving force in your life.

EXAMINE YOURSELF

Heed the Call!

Here are some of the calls Jesus gave to us in His ministry. The only way we can obey His call is to be empowered by the Holy Spirit. Read each call, and then ask the Holy Spirit to empower that call in your walk.

> I have been given complete authority in heaven and on earth. Therefore, go and make disciples of all the nations, baptizing them in the name of the Father and the Son and the Holy Spirit. Teach these new disciples to obey all the commands I have given you. And be sure of this: I am with you always, even to the end of the age. (MATT. 28:18–20)

> Go into all the world and preach the Good News to everyone, everywhere . . . These signs will accompany those who believe: They will cast out demons in my name, and they will speak new languages. They will be able to handle snakes with safety, and if they drink anything poisonous, it won't hurt them. They will be able to place their hands on the sick and heal them. (MARK 16:15–18)

With my authority, take this message of repentance to all the nations, beginning in Jerusalem: "There is forgiveness of sins for all who turn to me." You are witnesses of all these things. And now I will send the Holy Spirit, just as my Father promised. But stay here in the city until the Holy Spirit comes and fills you with power from heaven. (LUKE 24:47–49)

Write a prayer asking the Holy Spirit which part of these commissions He wants to empower you to do right now.

_____

OBEYING THE CALL

Ask the Holy Spirit for Guidance and Direction

How is the Holy Spirit guiding you each day to obey Jesus' commission to go into all the world? What is He telling you to do? Complete these sentences:

The Spirit is guiding me to _____

One way He is helping me fulfilling Jesus' commission is _____

OBEY THE SPIRIT

What Must You Do?

The Holy Spirit compels us to obey Jesus. What is the Holy Spirit compelling you to do in obedience to the call of Christ? Write down what He is commanding you to do.

_____

Day 5: Keep On Walking in the Spirit

The Holy Spirit is your constant Counselor, Companion, Comforter, and Friend. He is the Spirit of truth revealing everything to you. Use today to reflect on all that you have experienced from the Holy Spirit. Complete these sentences:

I experienced the breath of God's Spirit when _____

I experienced the leading of God's Spirit_____

I know the Spirit is acting in my life by_____

The fruit of the Spirit in my life are manifested by_____

The gifts of the Spirit that operate through me powerfully are _____

_____

I have experienced the gifts of_____

I experience the indwelling presence of the Holy Spirit _____

_____

The Holy Spirit is purifying and making me holy by_____

_____

The Holy Spirit convicts me by _____

_____

I flow in the Spirit when _____

_____

I experience the Spirit's miracles, signs, and wonders_____

_____

I am anointed by the Spirit_____

_____

When I pray in the Spirit _____

_____

I hear and obey the Spirit telling me to _____

_____

 Write a prayer thanking Jesus for giving you the Holy Spirit.

_____

_____

Appendix: POINTERS FOR LEADERS

1. This workbook can be used in the following settings:

    • Sunday school classes

    • Small groups

    • Cell and home groups

    • Bible study groups

    • Special studies for men, women, or young people

2. Before the meeting, the group leader and participants should have completed all of the daily studies. If participants do not complete the daily studies, they will have very little to share in the group sessions.

3. Group sessions should be no longer than about ninety minutes in length and could begin with a time of praise and worship, prayer, or a combination of both.

4. Before the participants gather, the leader should pray in the Spirit for each session and listen to the leading of the Holy Spirit concerning what will happen in each session.

5. Before the session, the group leader needs to select portions from each lesson for sharing as led by the Spirit. Use about half of the time sharing what the participants learned from studying the Scriptures and the other half of the time with the participants sharing how they experienced the Holy Spirit during the week.

6. During the session, ask everyone to share something concerning each exercise from the daily studies that the leader has chosen for discussion.

7. Group size should be limited to no more than twelve to fifteen people for optimal sharing.

8. Take time at the end of the group session for participants to pray for one another. This ministry time is very important for allowing the Holy Spirit to move freely in the group.

9. Start the session on time, and if the ministry time at the end of each session goes beyond the total time of ninety minutes for the whole session, then allow people to leave and attend to other responsibilities.

10. Remember that this is not a therapy group. If group members seek to dominate, manipulate, or control the group, speak with them outside the group session about how their behavior is hindering the work of the Holy Spirit in the group.